The Praying Church

SUE CURRAN

Published by Treasure House: 1995

Treasure House

An Imprint of

Destiny Image Publishers, Inc.®
P.O. Box 310
Shippensburg, PA 17257-0310

"For where your treasure is
there will your heart be also." Matthew 6:21

ISBN 1-56043-250-0

For Worldwide Distribution
Printed in the U.S.A.

Treasure House books are available through these fine distributors outside the United States:

Christian Growth, Inc.
Jalan Kilang-Timor, Singapore 0315

Vine Christian Centre
Mid Glamorgan, Wales, United Kingdom

Rhema Ministries Trading
Randburg, South Africa

Vision Resources
Ponsonby, Auckland, New Zealand

Salvation Book Centre
Petaling, Jaya, Malaysia

WA Buchanan Company
Geebung, Queensland, Australia

Successful Christian Living
Capetown, Rep. of South Africa

Word Alive
Niverville, Manitoba, Canada

Inside the U.S., call toll free to order:
1-800-722-6774

This book is lovingly dedicated to the church at Shekinah—co-laborers with me in the Gospel. Our years of experience together in prayer formed the background from which the concepts for this book were drawn.

Acknowledgements

I wish to acknowledge the faithfulness and diligence of Betsy Nelson in assisting me in the preparation of the manuscript. Her suggestions for clarity of expression are greatly appreciated, as well as her cheerful encouragement during the writing process.

My thanks to Brenda McGraw for technical writing and her dedication to the book's purpose, and to Wolfgang Wendland for his computer expertise.

Julie Bland, Carol Heimbach, and Carol Noe have done very capable work proofing the text. My appreciation to Cheryl Tipon for her editing skills.

And to my sister, Glenna Adams, and my nephew, Nick Adams, many thanks for their contribution to the layout of the book.

I gratefully acknowledge the assistance, encouragement, and fine abilities of all these who gladly offered their services and support.

Foreword

The theology of prayer has been with the Church from her early beginnings. The value of prayer has been preached again and again; our responsibility to pray has been heralded until most Christians live in a failure complex about their prayer lives, which keeps them from wanting to read a book on prayer because they fear it will only increase their load of guilt. Quite honestly, we give lip service to prayer far more than we give our lips to the service of prayer. We talk about prayer more than we talk to God in prayer.

While our spirits yearn for the intimate fellowship with God that prayer offers, our souls rebel at the discipline required to enter into that communion. Like the dieter who just cannot maintain the necessary self-control to lose weight, so we Christians fall into and out of prayer patterns with disappointing regularity. Is it possible that we need the undergirding help of others who are facing the same conflict? If Weight Watchers can help dieters and

Alcoholics Anonymous can assist problem drinkers back to a life of sobriety, isn't it possible that corporate prayer could help believers take and maintain the step out of the guilt of prayerlessness into the glory of a life of prayer?

This happened at Shekinah. I knew this congregation before it entered into corporate prayer; I watched the people closely while they were initiating corporate prayer; and I have shared in the continuing benefits of their unbroken corporate praying. Sue Curran, director of Shekinah Ministries, is a dear friend of mine, and she is both a praying woman and an innovator. She dares to believe that Bible principles are practical and workable. She consistently approaches the situations that arise in her congregation from the dual posture of being a student of the Word and a communicant with God. As a result, her leadership is scriptural, practical, and communicable. This book is a fine example of this fact. It does not preach "Do this," but it consistently testifies, "We did this, because God's Word says to, and these are the results." All Christian leaders need to review the principles expounded in this book.

Judson Cornwall, Th.D.
Phoenix, Arizona
March 1987

Contents

PART FIVE

Author's Preface

Many volumes have been written on the subject of individual, personal prayer. Spiritual giants such as David Brainerd, Rees Howells, John Hyde, and Edward Payson have awed us with their gifting and motivation to spend hours daily in intercession. E. M. Bounds, A. J. Gordon, and others have inspired us with their profound teachings on various aspects of prayer. Revival historians such as Edwin Orr have chronicled prayer movements, such as the great prayer revival of 1858-1859.

In contrast to this vast offering, practical instruction on corporate praying appears extremely scarce. Yet this is the day that God is calling His people all over the world to pray together. Thousands are gathering for the early morning hour of prayer. Churches of every size and description are being drawn to satisfy the heart of the Father as their people respond, "... early will I seek Thee ..." (Psalm 63:1).

In the spring of 1980, a revival released the

keys of corporate prayer to a pastor and congregation. Through a sovereign move of the Holy Spirit, the church found itself in prayer as a body morning and evening, day after day, week after week. When, after four months, the intensity of this great move of prayer and repentance subsided, it was as if a mighty wave had rolled in. And in the wake of that wave there remained a corporate prayer life established by the leadership of the Spirit Himself, teaching, as no man could, the way of God in corporate communion.

Prayer is not new, nor is the willingness of individuals to give themselves to it. But the *prayer meeting*, long the stepchild of the Church, is again finding its place of honor as many churches are meeting at appointed times, some every morning or several evenings weekly. These meetings for prayer are not intended to replace private times of prayer, family devotions, or other individual efforts, but God is placing a special blessing in the midst of those who have exercised the privilege and power of corporate prayer. This book is about that blessing and how to enter into it.

Part One

Principles and Precedents

Principles and Precedents

Introduction

A study of corporate prayer naturally finds its genesis in the Scriptures, which are the basis for all expressions in the life of God's Church. As we search the Scriptures, we discover that the Lord employs two methods of transmitting His truth to His people: through teaching and by example. These *principles* and *precedents* form the foundation of our understanding of what His Church is to be in the earth.

We are admonished to "approve ourselves unto the Lord" by "rightly dividing" His Word (II Timothy 2:15). By examining God's teaching on a subject and carefully analyzing the recorded responses of His people, we prepare ourselves to appreciate and cooperate with His movings among us today. The Lord does not change. His principles are eternal. By understanding His ways, we "approve ourselves" unto the Lord to fulfill His Kingdom purposes.

The reality of corporate prayer involves an

understanding of the unity and fellowship of the saints—the functioning of the church as the body of Christ. The following passage from Hebrews describes the basic elements of our corporate life:

> This is the covenant I will make with them after that time, says the Lord. I will put my laws in their hearts, and I will write them on their minds. . . . Therefore, brothers, since we have confidence to enter the Most Holy Place by the blood of Jesus . . . let us draw near to God with a sincere heart in full assurance of faith . . . And let us consider how we may spur one another on toward love and good deeds. Let us not give up meeting together as some are in the habit of doing, but let us encourage one another and all the more as you see the day approaching (Hebrews 10:15-24, NIV).

This passage outlines the process of our being built into spiritual houses—or churches: 1) the *covenant* makes God's teachings (laws) live in our hearts; 2) the *entrance* is made, by Jesus' blood, to the Father for relationship and answered prayer; 3) *corporate communion* maintains the vitality of the Kingdom purpose.

A church participating in the life of God's Kingdom on earth must continue to grow and develop in all of these aspects. The expansion of our revelation of God and the deepening of our relationship with Him as a people must find a commensurate maturing in our corporate expressions. God expects the prayer life of a church to grow, to change, in the same way a body of believers matures in other aspects of its spiritual life.

When Shekinah began in 1973, the Lord inspired us to take a real step of faith in buying 160 acres. He led us to build a conference center and develop a Christian community to support a base of operations for the ministry He desired us to enter. Prayer was not an option. We had taken such a step of faith in relation to our size that we *had* to pray to preserve what we had!

As the work continued to grow, our prayer lives also had to grow in measure with His blessing. By 1979 I was sensing a real need for our people to be established in prayer. We had always had the standard of giving at least an hour a day to the Lord in prayer, and the church leadership prayed together often. I personally would spend the first half of each morning in prayer. But we desired to see the Lord move among us in Holy Ghost revival. So I began to teach on revival, both from the pulpit and in our Bible college. For a full year, every Saturday night I taught the whole church on prayer and then we would divide into small groups to pray. In looking back, we must admit that some of those prayer meetings were a trial! But we had to start somewhere, and we came to know what to ask of the Lord in this regard.

One Sunday morning in late February of 1980, we experienced a powerful move of the Holy Spirit in our church service. We set aside the next week to pray and fast, planning to meet morning, afternoon, and evening. But the Lord came in such power that the morning prayer meeting ran into the afternoon prayer meeting, which ran into the evening meeting!

The Holy Spirit remained with us in this intensity for three months. Many of us prayed throughout each day and the whole church gathered for prayer every evening. God melted our hearts. He brought us to repentance. He gave us faith for the ministries He opened for us. He brought people from the nations of the earth to us and allowed us to minister to them the realities of prayer and revival.

Spending that period of time in the presence of the Lord brought us into a realm of prayer that the devil has never been able to take away from us. God made us into a *house of prayer.* In the aftermath of that experience, we have seen the value of the year of preparation that preceded the Lord's visitation. Our study of the principles and precedents of corporate prayer in the Scriptures and through Church history enlarged our capacity to receive and assimilate His intense move among us, inspiring and challenging us to press into the great privilege of corporate prayer.

1

The Principle of Agreement

Foundational Teaching on Corporate Prayer

Through His teachings, Jesus unfolded the Father's plan for His Kingdom. He taught His followers what the Kingdom was like and how to enter into it. In the same manner, He responded to His disciples' requests to teach them to pray. On several occasions He taught them *what* to pray, the most noted example being the model prayer commonly called the Lord's prayer. But Jesus also gave His followers much instruction in *how* to pray. In Matthew 18 He instituted the *prayer ministry of the church,* introducing the concept of *agreement* in prayer.

> Again I say unto you, that if two of you shall agree on earth as touching anything that they shall ask, it shall be done for them of my Father which is in heaven (Matthew 18:19).

This is much more than a promise of His faithfulness to those who are willing to join together to get their prayers answered; it is the institution of the Father's plan to bring the church together to pray. The reward is almost too good to be true: "If you shall agree on . . . anything . . . it shall be done. . . ."

THE POWER OF AGREEMENT

I believe Jesus' point was far more than simply getting us to pray together. His *emphasis* was on agreement, which is impossible with fewer than two. The *purpose* of that agreement was to energize our praying. It is clear from this passage of Scripture that a special power is promised through corporate prayer. We can deduce, then, that God will do things through the agreeing prayers of the church that He does not do through individual efforts. The power of our agreement in prayer *on earth* brings a response from the Father *in heaven*. Heaven is waiting for earth to ask in agreement!

Furthermore, verse 18 of Matthew 18 teaches us that the awesome power to bind and loose is given to the praying church. The wonder is that heaven answers to earth and that God entrusts this power to the church that is praying in agreement.

The prayer ministry of the church accomplishes much. The prayer gathering enlarges the channel through which God will bless and give victory to His people; it actually moves us into an entirely different realm of power. Two Old Testament Scriptures provide a picture of the power Jesus promised in collective praying:

> And five of you shall chase an hundred, and an hundred of you shall put ten thousand to flight (Leviticus 26:8).

> How should one chase a thousand, and two put ten thousand to flight, except their Rock had sold them, and the Lord had shut them up? (Deuteronomy 32:30).

My husband, John, worked as a mathematician and scientist before coming into the ministry. I asked him to chart on a piece of graph paper the number that two hundred praying people could put to flight, based on the equations introduced in the above Scriptures. He told me it couldn't be done—the calculations would run off the page! The power that God gives in corporate agreement explodes our finite comprehensions.

When we move from praying alone to praying corporately, we move into a realm in which results are calculated exponentially. We move from the realm of addition to that of multiplication: for every person added, the prayer power is multiplied. Corporate agreement is the key to *exponential power* in prayer.

Understanding the power of agreement revolutionizes our expectations in prayer. But the concept of agreement entails conditions we must meet before the power can flow.

The Prerequisite of Agreement

"If two agree. . . ." This Greek word is suggestive of our English word *symphony.* Jesus was speaking of a symphony or concert of prayer. The instruments and parts vary, but everyone is playing the same piece. It is harmony, not cacophony.

Harmony is the element that makes corporate prayer work. This understanding goes beyond agreeing about the things for which we pray (see Chapter 8, "Keys to Corporate Prayer: Unity"). The real work of grace that brings the power of God is *harmony between the saints themselves.*

Jesus made two statements relative to this point: "For where two or three are gathered in my name, there am I in the midst of them" (Matthew 18:20); later He prayed to the Father "that they may be one, even as we are one" (John 17:22). The agreement Jesus seeks is of the heart, not of words in prayer. The flesh may not always detect lack of agreement, but the Spirit censors it in the heavenly realm.

Jesus taught us that the shortest way to God is by the house of our offended brother (Matthew 5:23,24). We are not to offer our prayers until we are reconciled to—are in agreement with—our brother. Those unwilling to do this hinder the agreeing power of the prayer effort.

When God came to our congregation in sovereign revival, the first area with which He dealt with us was attitudes of unforgiveness and irreconciliation. He required us to forgive everyone—to *continually* forgive and ask for forgiveness. If we refused to be truly reconciled to one another, He withdrew His Spirit until we obeyed. In response to this understanding, we have determined through the power of Jesus to live our lives in agreement with one another.

Surely we hear commanding voices to bind and loose raised all around us. But heaven has promised to answer only the *agreeing* voices of the church. The power is not in the commanding, but in our obedience to be an agreeing church.

2

More Than Answers

Rewards of Corporate Prayer

We have learned that sincere prayer not only produces answers; it also reaps rewards: "... thy Father ... shall reward thee ..." (Matthew 6:6). The prayer meeting is a place of asking and receiving rewards beyond our asking.

TRUST—A STRENGTH AGAINST THE ENEMY

As the Spirit has led our church into corporate prayer, we have learned that "eye has not seen nor ear heard what God has prepared for us." A previously unknown love and unity has been built among us. As we have confessed our faults and received forgiveness from God and our brothers (James 5:16), a divine trust has developed which has formed a strong weapon against the enemy and a wall of loyalty that is almost impossible to penetrate. The result is a strength which has established us defensively as well as offensively against the forces of satan.

CONFESSION AND CLEANSING

We have found the corporate prayer meeting to be a fountainhead for cleansing and healing of the soul through repentance. How much unnecessary suffering results from sins that build up in the congregation until they seem insurmountable. Condemnation then paralyzes the church until she sinks into discouraged inertia. The discouraged man never does anything for God! The transparent life of corporate prayer keeps us honest before one another, removing the stifling blanket of condemnation.

THE SCHOOL OF PRAYER

The prayer meeting also becomes the school of prayer. Those inexperienced in prayer are trained by the example of mature pray-ers, while all are stirred and inspired through agreement with powerful prayer expressions. Even our younger children (ages three to six) know how to construct a prayer and speak it boldly. This is the result of their having attended the school of prayer on such a regular basis. Inhibitions have been dealt with by the

Holy Spirit so that fear is a relative stranger in our meetings for prayer.

CHANNEL FOR REVELATION

We have seen the body ministry (I Corinthians 12) in action as individual members of the prayer meeting have supplied the needs of one another, especially through revelation out of God's Word. That which is revealed to one becomes the possession of all as a truth is shared in the meeting. The whole body together becomes a channel for revelation, as a huge water pipe, large enough to carry the full stream of the Lord's blessing. To one the Lord might make alive a truth about the sin of pride. To another He might give a deeper understanding of the atonement. Yet another might uncover a device of the enemy. Faith for healing in one seems to spark faith for it in another. What is truly quickened by the Spirit to one can be claimed by all. Still others can pray or sing our own heart's desires. Our personal expressions Godward are enriched and enlarged when offered in concert with others. Then we understand how "the eye cannot say to the hand, I have no need of thee" (I Corinthians 12:21).

A fresh understanding of Scripture, a prophetic word, a deliverance from bondage becomes the reward of all who are present as we share in the blessing God pours through a chosen channel. We begin to see ourselves as vessels which God uses to bless the whole. There is an expectation that God would speak to each of us in the prayer meetings. We drink from a much deeper well because we drink together.

3

The Business of Life

Priority of Corporate Prayer

As we come to appreciate the awesome benefits and power of corporate praying, we can better understand why Jesus implemented this kind of praying by command. Among the last words spoken before He departed this earth were those in Acts 1:4: "Wait for the promise of the Father. ..." Verse 14 of Acts 1 shows that the people understood *wait* to mean that they were to *continue in prayer*. One hundred and twenty did exactly that.

THE ACTS EXAMPLE

How we stand in admiration and amazement as we read the chapters that follow! But it began with a prayer meeting, and the movement continued to draw its impetus from the believers' great commitment to prayer. The enemy never ceases in his endeavor to keep us from prayer for he knows that if a work is not founded on a great prayer effort, it lacks the power to stand in times of attack and shaking. If we are not praying, satan has already succeeded in deceiving us about the work of prayer.

The Acts church was not deceived. They did not see an "imbalance" in their engaging in prayer so much of the time. Acts 2:46 says they were "continuing daily with one accord in the temple." Peter and John were on their way to a prayer meeting when they healed the lame man (Acts 3). A prayer meeting in which "they lifted up their voice to God with one accord" (Acts 4:24) produced a literal shaking of the house in which they prayed (verse 31), followed by an infilling of the Holy Ghost. Peter was miraculously delivered from prison through the prayers of the gathered saints (Acts 12:5-11).

Obedience to Jesus' command and adherence to His teaching relating to the power of praying together launched the early Church into a pattern of prayer that greatly affected their lifestyle. The same Spirit that came on the day of Pentecost is again filling us with holy longings. Like the believers in Acts, those responding to the Spirit in this day will make prayer the great business of life.

THE PRAYER PRIORITY

In every description of the early Church, we find the believers *continuing* in prayer:

> Those all continued with one accord in prayer and supplication (Acts 1:14).

> And they continued steadfastly in the apostles' doctrine and fellowship, and breaking of bread, and in prayers (Acts 2:42).

> Continue in prayer (Colossians 4:2).

Throughout the New Testament instruction and commands concerning prayer include this same word: ". . . continuing instant in prayer" (Romans 12:12).

In all these Scriptures, the Greek word for "continue" is *proskartereo,* which means "to be in constant readiness or give constant attention to a thing." Though not in reference to prayer, its use in Mark 3:9 paints a graphic picture as to its application: "And he spake to his disciples that a small ship should wait on him because of the multitude, lest they should throng him." The word "continuing" in the other Scriptures is here translated "wait on." The boat was ready for Jesus to keep the people from crowding Him. The idea is that the boat had been prepared and marked: "Jesus' purpose has first priority." That boat had been set aside for His purposes. It was not to be considered for anything else.

So *proskartereo,* as concerning prayer means to be in constant readiness, to wait continually, or to have as a first purpose. The first work of the Kingdom is prayer. The early church made prayer their priority. Their prayer lives dictated their lifestyle so that they might accomplish the Word of God. Likewise, if we are going to fulfill the commands of Jesus, we must make prayer the business of our lives. Such an attitude will preclude many of the pitfalls that sabotage our prayer lives. If prayer is our business, we are not dependent upon "feelings." How many people go to work only when they feel like it? We won't "bottom out" if we pray from principle rather than from sensation.

A regular prayer life demands dedication and discipline. People move away from prayer to please their flesh, and the devil provides the perfect excuse for them: "Organized prayer is legalism!" "Legalistic" is the devil's misinterpretation of "faithful." If prayer is our first occupation, then the prayer meeting becomes the place of greatest fulfillment and opportunity of expression.

With prayer as the business of life, we eliminate the tired refrain "I don't have time to pray!" If we are too busy to offer God more than occasional ejaculatory prayers, then we must admit that our lives are tied up with all kinds of things that are *not* the business of life. If we evaluate our lifestyles honestly, in the end we must conclude that *we* choose what will be in them.

God does not want to crowd our lives with prayer. Prayer is a place to take our leisure in Him. It is to be a refuge from the chaos of the world. In prayer, in His presence, we follow the admonition for life in Psalm 34:12,14: "What man is he who desireth life, and loveth many days, that he may see good? Depart from evil, and do good; seek peace, and pursue it." The Prince of Peace reigns in the place of prayer. The prayer meeting becomes our point of contact for entering into the rest He has promised (Hebrews 4:9-11).

The Lord apprehended us with this challenging thought: we find time to be at leisure for our pleasure, but do we diligently *take* time to be at leisure for His pleasure? For example, early morning prayer requires that we reorganize our evenings. Our lifestyles will reflect our obedience to Jesus' commands. We make prayer a priority by rearranging our lives around our praying. Like the small boat the disciples prepared for Jesus, we bear the stamp "Jesus' purpose has first priority."

4

The Fruit and Its Root

Historical Testimony of Corporate Prayer

The Church's call to corporate prayer is evident from the place of its origin: a prayer meeting on the day of Pentecost. God's challenge comes to pastors and other leaders to articulate this call to their congregations and inspire them to this great privilege of corporate prayer. Inevitably a conflict to this challenge will arise in the area of priorities. The question revolves around the concept of productivity—or, to use the scriptural term, "fruit-bearing."

STRENGTH IN WAITING

Christ's expression of the Father's intention for Christians—"I have chosen you and ordained you, that ye should go and bring forth fruit and that your fruit should remain" (John 15:16)—stands as the evidence or mark of the effectiveness of His Church in the earth. The

41

usual emphasis of the Church is on production—accomplishing things *for God*. The vital prerequisite we often miss is that production must be preceded by conception—the branch must abide in the vine prior to bearing fruit.

Quite often studies of Church history focus on the result of production rather than on the source of conception. Of course our ultimate source of life is in God Himself; yet there is a necessary principle at work: the Church must receive *strength* to conceive in order to produce. The key to this working is found in the familiar passage in Isaiah 40:31: "They that *wait upon* the Lord shall renew their strength." A call to corporate prayer is a call to wait upon the Lord. Strength, conception, and ultimately the production of lasting fruit issue from this primary waiting.

Our "production-oriented" mentality must be refocused to embrace the foundational element of prayer involved in bearing fruit that remains. Convincing a congregation of this necessity may appear to the earnest pastor to be a considerable challenge. But the One who mediates between challenge and conflict is the Holy Spirit. "Thy people shall be willing in the day of Thy power" (Psalm 110:3) is God's promise that He will provide a means of persuading His people.

We may look to Church history for inspiration and testimony of God's power to birth entire congregations into the realm of Spirit-led prayer. Revival (a "re-lifing" of believers) and evangelism/missions (the conversion of the lost) have been the measure of the Church's productivity through the centuries. If our ultimate goal is to bear fruit in God's Kingdom, we would do well to discover the historical sources for revival and evangelism.

THE MORAVIANS

On August 13, 1727, a group of European believers called Moravians were visited by the Holy Spirit in their regular morning prayer meeting. One biographer wrote, "They left the house of God hardly knowing whether they belonged to earth or had already gone to heaven."[1] The Moravian movement was birthed and continued to proliferate through the power of unceasing prayer. The initial visitation established a corporate prayer life for the Moravians that they maintained for over a hundred years. This relatively small (several hundred) praying band accomplished more in the arena of world missions in twenty years than had been accomplished by the evangelical Church in the preceding two centuries.

As they prayed, the spirit of prayer came to dwell with them. While the Holy Spirit is the power to persuade us to pray, we must also consider man's part in God's working. Spurgeon's successor, A. T. Pierson said,

> From the day of Pentecost there has not been one great awakening in any land which has not yet begun in a union of prayer, though only by two or three; no such outward and upward movement has continued after such prayer meetings have declined; and it is in direct proportion to the maintenance of such joint and believing supplication and intercession that the Word of the Lord in any land or in any locality has had free course and been glorified.[2]

Thus we have a sacred paradox: the Holy Spirit inspires prayer; prayer opens the way for the Holy Spirit to move.

Our church spent one year praying for revival. When it came, we discovered a Person had come. That Person was the Holy Spirit. He brought with Him a desire for prayer that far exceeded what we had previously known. As we continued in established meetings for prayer, we opened the way for Him to continue His visitation with us.

A renewed interest in meetings for prayer is characteristic of revivals through the centuries. In fact, the meetings for prayer, more often than not, *are* the revival meetings. Preaching is oftentimes only incidental. The great revival of 1858 was a prayer revival. It began with a prayer meeting on September 23, 1857, where six men gathered. Soon revival had swept most of the nation, and flames began to ignite around the world. There was preaching, but it was greatly overshadowed by prayer.

Matthew Henry said, "When God intends great mercy for His peoples, the first thing He does is to set them a-praying."[3]

Notes

1. Oswald J. Smith, *The Enduement of Power* (London: Marshall, Morgan, & Scott, 1933), p. 112.
2. Quoted in Arthur Wallis, *Rain From Heaven* (Minneapolis, Minnesota: Bethany Fellowship, Inc., 1979), p. 115.
3. Oswald J. Smith, *The Enduement of Power* (London: Marshall, Morgan, & Scott, 1933), p. 112.

5

The Indispensable Example

Role of Leadership in Corporate Prayer

Jesus' prayer life was without doubt an inspiration to His disciples. There was stirred in them a desire to learn to pray as He did (Luke 11:1). Certain blessed individuals in a church will have a special gifting of prayer. But the challenge before churches today is to bring the *whole* congregation to a true desire to pray. This must begin with the visible dedication and zeal of the pastor for prayer. Then the pastor must communicate to his staff and other leaders this same dedication so that the church can be led by *example.*

Teaching on prayer is necessary, but unless the congregation knows that the pastor prays, and unless the pastor prays *with* the congregation, his teachings will not be convincing. Jesus first inspired by His own example. As a result, He had a willing audience for His teachings.

Often a pastor will turn the prayer meetings

over to his assistants and elders while he does other things that "only he can do." Such actions subtly make the statement that those "other things" are more important than prayer. If he allows pressing counseling sessions or administrative details to have priority over prayer, he is exalting these to his congregation. The congregation will neither revere prayer nor make it a priority beyond the standard set by the pastor.

The disciples established themselves as men of prayer when they handed down their decision to the early Church (Acts 6). Others could care for the temporal needs of the people; they would give themselves continually to prayer and to the ministry of the Word (verses 2-4). Notice the results of this decision in verse 7: "And the word of God increased; and the number of the disciples multiplied . . . greatly."

In his teachings on prayer, Charles Finney, that great American revivalist, said that prayer meetings are the most difficult meetings to sustain because they are the most spiritual meetings of the church.[1] My own conviction formed from personal experience and considerable study of revival history is that the pastor's example must be the initiating force in the prayer ministry of the church. Further, the success of such ministry greatly depends upon the spirituality and ability of strong leadership in corporate prayer. (See Part Five for expansion of this subject.)

So often it seems that God in His mercy will give a church two or three saints who love God and understand prayer enough to keep that church afloat even when the pastor and congregation have no prayer life to speak of. Such a church can never make any truly significant gains in the Kingdom purpose, for what little prayer effort that is expended operates in the realm of survival—hanging on rather than going forward.

But for the many for whom survival is not enough, Jesus left a plan—a plan of purpose and a plan of power. Prayer is both the law and the work of the Kingdom.

Note

1. Charles Grandison Finney, *Finney on Revival* (Minneapolis, Minnesota: Bethany Fellowship, Inc.), p. 54.

Part Two

The Corporate Expression

The Corporate Expression

Introduction

Henry Ward Beecher said, "He who can take a parish and develop in it a good prayer-meeting, carry it on through years and still have it fruitful, various, spiritual,—he is a general."[1] The pastor should not feel alone who has experienced numerous or overwhelming difficulties in his effort to establish prayer meetings, even to the point of having been defeated. People must become educated in the practical aspects of corporate prayer. We need to understand what things might defeat the meeting and conversely, what are the greatest helps. There are ways of inspiring and motivating to prayer and some methods are more successful than others. Certain attitudes and mentalities need to be adjusted. ". . . the spirit indeed is willing, but the flesh is weak" (Matthew 26.41). There is value and help in considering the practical aspects of the prayer meeting.

Note

1. Henry Ward Beecher, *Yale Lectures on Preaching* (New York: Fords, Howard, and Hulbert, 1893), Second Series, p. 82.

6

Having the Spirit of Prayer

The Catalyst of Corporate Prayer

And because ye are sons, God hath sent forth the Spirit of his Son into your hearts crying, Abba, Father (Galatians 4:6).

Likewise the Spirit also helpeth our infirmities: for we know not what we should pray for as we ought: but the Spirit itself maketh intercession for us with groanings which cannot be uttered. And he that searcheth the hearts knoweth what is the mind of the Spirit, because he maketh intercession for the saints according to *the will of God* (Romans 8:26-27, emphasis added).

The Holy Spirit within us prays to the Father so that we can pray according to the will of God. This spirit of prayer (or Spirit-led praying) is the foundation of the corporateness of the prayer meeting. The power of corporate prayer is not in many people praying with each other, but in the uniting of many hearts with the Spirit of God to pray the mind and will of the Father.

The life of the prayer meeting, as well as the direction the meeting takes, is dependent upon the release of the spirit of prayer. There is no great mystery to flowing in the spirit of prayer: one simply allows the Holy Spirit to pray through him. The key to this abandonment to the Spirit is sensitivity. Such sensitivity is cultivated by time spent meditating in God's Word, in worship, and in private prayer—in essence, by exposure to the presence of God.

Spiritual sensitivity is communicated as we gather for prayer. Those acknowledging their need for greater spirituality in prayer should join themselves with other gifted pray-ers. In this way they can become infected with a "holy contagion." The corporate prayer meeting itself becomes the avenue for growth in the spirit of prayer.

This is perhaps the most wonderful aspect of the spirit of prayer: it is contagious! Charles Finney said, "Nothing is more calculated to beget a spirit of prayer than to unite in social prayer with one who has the Spirit himself."[1] The astonishing economy of God's Kingdom is again displayed, for the corporate prayer meeting is at the same time both the school and work place of prayer.

As a person allows the Spirit to pray through

him, the whole gathering can be lifted into the realm of the spirit of prayer. Others should defer to the one being used in this way at a given time. Those who are born again have no difficulty discerning the prayer of the Spirit. They will be quickened to pray by the Spirit as a result of the catalytic effect of the anointed prayer.

Once the spirit of prayer has established an emphasis in a prayer meeting, others should exercise caution in changing the subject or direction without a definite leading of the Spirit. Generally speaking, we should pray through on a subject until the level of faith for it has been exhausted. Successive prayers build the level of faith. Elements of inspiration, revelation, desire, and agreement allow us to "ride" the currents of faith to a certain end.

We must lay aside our natural inclinations and reasonings and submit to the leadership of the Holy Spirit. If someone unwittingly diverts the course the Spirit has set, the leader should return the meeting to the proper subject or direction as smoothly as possible. The power of the spirit of prayer delivers us from aimless praying to focus on the will and purposes of God for each prayer gathering.

Varying degrees of intensity of the spirit of prayer will be present in prayer meetings. Though we cannot produce the spirit of prayer of ourselves, God's promise is to send the Holy Spirit to assist us each time we present ourselves as willing vessels. Our goal should be to make ourselves wholly available to God, for only as the Spirit has His way is the purpose of gathering for prayer accomplished.

Note

1. Charles Grandison Finney, *Finney on Revival* (Minneapolis, Minnesota: Bethany Fellowship, Inc.), p. 52.

7

Overcoming the Obstacles

Ten Hindrances to Corporate Prayer

Prayer is the work of the Kingdom. Prayer meetings are the most spiritual and spiritually demanding meetings of the church, so they are the most difficult meetings to sustain. They have two enemies: the flesh and the devil. Finney said, "The devil has no conscience and the flesh has no sense."[1] Our greatest mistake is to allow these difficulties to discourage the prayer effort.

Satan has a plan to keep us from praying, and the flesh is too insensitive to the Spirit to understand its own destructive power. Together this pilfering pair has succeeded in putting to sleep or to death many promising prayer efforts. Such difficulties are actually hurdles to be surmounted on our journey to being established as a praying church.

The role of leadership in the prayer meeting is essential to the meeting's success. Without strong leadership, the flesh and the devil will systematically undermine the work of the Spirit. The role of the leader is to keep the prayer meeting on course. This is not a job for the easily discouraged or the impractical person.

When individuals unwittingly become involved in hindering the prayer meeting by the manner in which they pray, it is the responsibility of the leader to give instruction or gentle correction. It is important to understand that sincere people, valuable to the Kingdom purpose, sometimes are insensitive or untaught regarding corporate prayer. These people will welcome instruction, as their intention is to contribute to the prayer effort. The person who is unwilling to receive scriptural correction will not lend himself to the unity so necessary for powerful corporate praying.

Now, let us extract by way of example, ten of the most common fleshly hindrances to corporate prayer.

(1) Teaching Prayers.   True praying is "pouring out your heart before him" (Psalm 62:8). That is prayer from a sincere motive. But there is also the prayer of the one who has a point to make or some understanding he feels is too valuable to keep to himself. In his enthusiam he spills his mind to the people, rather than pouring out his heart to God. He has not learned the purpose of prayer. A response to this problem is to simply tell the congregation, "Don't teach in your prayers. Pour out your hearts to God!"

(2) Controlling Prayers. A near relative of teaching prayers, controlling prayers bring the group under the direction of a self-appointed leader. Often others are not aware the leadership has changed, but the spiritual level of the meeting soon reveals something has happened. Should this occur, those in leadership should gently redirect the flow of the meeting Godward.

(3) Doctrinal/Attitudinal Prayers. These are similar to both teaching and controlling prayers, operating in a more religious vein. The prayer corrects the doctrine or intention of others. For instance, if someone has just repented and the person praying has chosen something "higher," he might pray, "Lord, we thank you that we have already repented. There is no condemnation. You did it all on Calvary and we're walking in the victory." When this happened in the revival at our church, the person involved was asked privately not to interfere in this way and to leave the direction of the meeting to the leadership of the church. By taking this responsibility, we enabled the people to continue in a sovereign move of God to cleanse and free us from our sins. People should be taught to flow with the approach of the leadership in such matters.

(4) Emotional Prayers.   Wild exuberance or hysterical wailing can kill a prayer meeting. God is displeased when a person moves into the realm of unreality. The key is discernment. Both joy and weeping can be a part of an "alive" prayer meeting, but a person is releasing his personality when he unburdens his feelings at the meeting's expense. Emotional expressions may be released, but only God-ward. When the one praying draws attention to himself, he is not drawing others into God's presence—he is damaging the prayer meeting.

(5) Morbid, Unbelieving Prayers.   Prayer is not a "pity party." People must be taught that however great or distressing their needs are, God has promised to respond to faith. While it may be acceptable within the context of the meeting to honestly weep and ask for God's intervention, it is always unbelief to simply express fear and depression. Often an appropriate song can lift a meeting that has fallen under the pall of unbelief. The goal is to kindle faith-filled attitudes.

(6) Striving Prayers.   Akin to the above-mentioned attitude, striving simply adds pride and energy to unbelief. The person doesn't really believe his prayer will be answered, and he thinks it is unfair that God is meeting others and not himself. Since he lacks faith, all he can really do is express his tension. Others will respond to the tension and assume his unbelieving posture without realizing it. Again, the prayer leaders must take the responsibility to set a positive tone for the meeting.

(7) Intellectual Prayers. The story is told of an old man who stood and prayed the same wool-gathering prayer, meeting after meeting. The prayer ended, "Lord, since last we met the cobwebs have again come between me and thee." Time after time a young man present was subjected to this meaningless praying until, unable to bear it any longer, he sprang to his feet and cried, "O God, kill the spider!" The intellectual pray-er has not learned about the spirit of prayer and performs rehearsed prayers of his own invention. It is in order to teach the people to "skip the adjectives" and to pour out their hearts before God.

(8) Dead Prayers. A cousin to intellectual prayers, these are usually spoken from throat level—never from the heart or even from the lungs. Though the prayer meeting can usually endure a few such "underwhelming" offerings without damage to the life of the meeting, people should be taught to pray from inspiration rather than from habit.

(9) Personal, Ambitious Prayers.   It is not wrong for a prayer to be personal, but there are persons who use public occasions to draw attention to themselves. They pray to be heard, to maintain their public image, or to impress the hearers with their potential for future leadership. Prayer should contribute to the direction the Spirit sets for the meeting.

(10) Uncooperative Prayers.   There will be those who must sit if everyone else is standing, pray quietly if everyone else is shouting, or read their Bibles if everyone else is praying. Then there is the person who "just doesn't feel like" singing and "just didn't get a witness" to that prophetic word (or the last fifteen). He is a hindrance. His opinion is more important to him than unity. Such "lone rangers" expose their lack of understanding concerning the body ministry.

When we recognize each of these ten just for what they are—hindrances to the prayer meeting—we are better equipped to deal with the unreal and offensive elements. Just as a highway engineer must clear the roadway of trees and other obstacles, so must we, in doing the work of the Kingdom, set ourselves free from these difficulties. Whenever possible, instruction and correction should be made in a general sense to the whole prayer gathering. The end of the prayer meeting is a good time to do this. If the problem pertains particularly to one person, it would be more kind to approach him privately.

Ephesians 4 tells us that the five-fold ministry is given to the Church for the perfecting (or preparing) of the saints to do the work of the ministry (verses 11,12). Instructing the saints in the manner of prayer is a part of this calling. Such ministry will bring us to unity and maturity. Instruction is vital for growth in the Kingdom purpose (verse 13).

Note

1. Noted in text but no information.

8

Unity, Faith, and Sincerity

Three Keys to Corporate Prayer

Unity, faith, and sincerity are the three keys to corporate prayer. Each of the ten hindrances in the previous chapter violates one of these three key elements. The operation of these keys safeguards the prayer effort from these hindrances and makes corporate prayer effective.

UNITY

Nowhere else in the life of the church is unity more vital than in corporate prayer, for it is as we are in *one accord* that the presence of God will come among us.

> ... they lifted up their voice to God with one accord ... And when they had prayed, the place was shaken where they were assembled together; and they were filled with the Holy Ghost ... (Acts 4:24,31).

> ... as the trumpeters and singers were as one, to make one sound to be heard in praising and thanking the Lord ... then the house was

filled with a cloud . . . for the glory of the Lord had filled the house of God (II Chronicles 5:13,14).

We have seen the necessity of agreement between the saints themselves; agreement also involves a uniting of our hearts in *desire, motive,* and *purpose* concerning the things for which we ask.

Desire.   Jesus said, "What things soever ye desire, when ye pray, believe that you shall receive them and ye shall have them" (Mark 11:24). Desire is a much stronger concept than saying, "I don't object." Our unity must spring from a fervent desire for that for which we are praying. The Lord examines our hearts beyond our words. Prayer is an activity of the heart, and corporate prayer is the uniting of hearts before God to receive what is earnestly desired.

Motive.   Once we unite in our desire, we must have the right reason for that desire! The only pure reason to pray is *for the glory of God.* Our motives cannot be clouded by personal ambition or selfishness or even human concern. God must approve of our desires and motives before He can answer our prayers. This requires a willingness for the Holy Spirit to continually examine our hearts and to purify our reasons for praying.

Purpose. Our purpose in prayer must be for *the will of God.* A unity springs from our willingness for God's will—whatever it is. This frees us from concepts that would limit the ways of God and we can join with others to embrace His moving without reservation. Thus unity creates an atmosphere of liberty in which the spirit of prayer can flow freely.

One Accord. Unity in corporate prayer also operates on a very practical level. Paul exhorts us to "make every effort to keep the unity of the Spirit through the bond of peace" (Ephesians 4:3). This understanding entails attitudes of deference, preferring one another in a spirit of cooperation. Our objective in corporate prayer is to project our prayers to the Father as "one man" (Ephesians 4:13).

Unity precludes attitudes that would seek to control a corporate prayer meeting, to draw attention through emotional extremes, or to be reluctant to cooperate with the direction of the meeting. Unity in heart reality and practicality preserves the corporateness that allows us to pray in one accord.

FAITH

The exercise of faith is particularly important when we consider corporate praying.

Jesus acknowledged that He did few mighty acts in his own region because of the community unbelief (Matthew 13:58). When He went to raise Jairus' daughter from the dead, He put all the unbelievers and scoffers out of the room!

Faith is a growing thing (II Corinthians 10:15), and it is our responsibility to provide a nurturing atmosphere. When enough unbelief is mixed with the prayers, there will be a neutralizing or negative effect, and as a result there will be very little answered prayer. This in turn discourages the people, causing them to suppose their prayers are of little value.

Sometimes there can come a religious satisfaction which says, "I have prayed," when actually one has only attended the prayer meeting. "Without faith it is impossible to please God" (Hebrews 11:6). We can pray without faith; thus, though we are praying we are still not pleasing God in our praying. This is not referring to amounts of faith—for we all vary in our levels of faith—but rather to the conscious decision to pray in faith and turn from unbelief and presumption.

At a point when we began to observe a waning interest in our church's early-morning prayer meetings, I assumed I should preach about prayer. When that did not bring change,

I tried to inspire the people to a disciplined life. But when I went to the Lord for an answer, my eyes were opened to see that we were lacking faith.

Faith expects great things of God. This expectation makes prayer exciting and challenging. When answers are seen, hearts are encouraged. The place of prayer has a renewed drawing on our lives. People need to know they are accomplishing something in prayer! Then they will look forward to being a part of that earthly base of operations that receives answers from heaven.

It's important to add that those who pray together must demonstrate faith for more than their specific prayer meeting. The way we conduct our lives should always be providing an atmosphere in which our faith can flourish. Negative and doubtful speaking will destroy our prayer lives. We must continually believe that God is, and that He is a rewarder of those who diligently seek Him (Hebrews 11:6). This is the basis of the life of faith.

One committed to the faith life has chosen and works at developing a mind-set for miracles. He accepts that God is a God who calls things that are not as though they are (Romans 4:17). He begins to pray with the attitude of expecting the miraculous. Once he knows how and what to pray, he begins to release his faith for the impossible. And miracles begin to happen!

SINCERITY

We are sincere when our actions accurately reflect our motives. Hypocrisy presents a facade which covers a wrong desire. The world calls this phony. The hypocrite in Matthew 6 loved to pray to be seen of men. A public prayer meeting is an ideal place for the hypocrite to perform.

Jesus gives a two-step cure for hypocritical praying: *Pray privately* and *pray to the Father* (verse 6). Obviously, this does not mean that we cease to gather for prayer, but rather that the man who prays *only* in public is a hypocrite. His motives are wrong.

If we learn to pray to the Father in secret, then we will also pray to Him in public. Though others are present, we pray to sincerely express our hearts to the Father and not to impress men. Much of our fear and reluctance involves this issue. A pure and sincere heart may be naturally shy, but in the prayer meeting it can forget the faces of men, for the Father is the object of its prayers. The woman with the alabaster box in Luke 7 was sincere, even though she violated the pharisaical protocol, and Jesus accepted her prayer.

One might say, "I don't want to go to pray today, so I should stay at home and not be a hypocrite." We all have days when our flesh would rather stay at home. To go and do our best to pray is sincerity.

Larry Lea (pastor of The Church on the Rock in Texas) teaches as the steps to learning to love prayer: From desire to discipline to delight. Desire results in discipline; discipline produces delight. The discipline stage represents the desire to overcome all obstacles and commune with God until it becomes a true delight. The interim is not hypocrisy but determination!

We would be wise to face squarely the propensity of our flesh to be hypocritical. Jesus' warning was not to the hypocrites who stood praying but to His followers who sat listening. If we pray in ways and tones to impress those present, we are hypocrites. If we are not sincere pray-ers, but attend prayer meetings for appearance' sake, we are hypocrites.

"And when thou prayest, thou shalt not be as the hypocrites . . ." (Matthew 6:5). In the same passage Jesus warns against vain repetitions (verses 7-8). Then follows what we have called the Lord's Prayer. It is an intelligent (not intellectual) pattern of praying in a sincere way for what we need and what God desires to do.

Attitudes long accepted as normal will need

to change as we give ourselves to corporate praying. Undoubtedly the eloquent pray-er who hides sin in his heart is a hypocrite. But so is the person who is so continually aware of those present that he has forgotten he came to pray to God!

The sincere pray-er throws off the yokes of fear and pride and joins his brothers and sisters in seeking the face of God with all his heart. Prayers need not be according to any preconceived or religious ideal, but they must be sincere. ". . . for the Lord seeth not as man seeth; for man looketh on the outward appearance, but the Lord looketh on the heart" (I Samuel 16:7).

9

The Prayer Meeting From Beginning to End

Practicalities of Corporate Prayer

Once we have committed ourselves to a spiritual unity and cooperation, we need to consider many practical aspects in facilitating corporate prayer. I am frequently asked about the "how-tos" of a church praying together. Many of the following examples are drawn from our experiences at Shekinah, but the information can be applied to a variety of situations. The intent is to communicate our experience in being led by the Lord, rather than to construct examples to be emulated. The prayer journey of each church is unique, with an original blueprint available only through the Holy Spirit.

THE PLACE

It is interesting to note that Jesus gave special attention to the *place* of gathering for the

Last Supper (Luke 22:10-12). The 120 gathered in an upper room set apart for prayer in preparation for the day of Pentecost. The location of the prayer meeting is important only in that it is a prepared place—a place free from distractions, a place that accommodates the needs of our mortal bodies.

Though used for other functions, our prayer room is always prepared beforehand by faithful ones who have undertaken this responsibility. The room can seat large or small gatherings with some space to walk and pray. We have found that arranging the chairs in concentric circles is conducive to including all.

Temperature control is especially important in large gatherings. Noise from hallways, air conditioners, etc., can overwhelm soft voices. Care in making the room comfortable and quiet creates an inviting atmosphere to "come apart" unto the Lord.

THE TIME

Attending prayer meetings will always be a matter of priorities—a sacrifice of self. Many churches, including ours, have found the 6:00 a.m. hour to be a previously unused time. Once the "battle of the bed" is won, setting this as an established time of corporate prayer is an unchallenged commitment.

We meet for prayer from 6:00-7:00 a.m. on weekdays and from 7:00-8:00 a.m. on weekends. This time has proved to be a special blessing for those who work full-time and so are otherwise unable to attend daytime prayer meetings.

Presently the Lord seems to be calling for this "firstfruits of the day" offering from His body around the world. We had already taught our congregation to spend an hour privately with the Lord upon rising each day. Thus the groundwork had previously been laid for moving into a corporate expression at this hour.

We also pray on Tuesdays and Thursdays at 8:30 a.m. These meetings are attended mostly by members without outside employment—staff members, mothers and small children, and Bible college students. Our largest corporate gathering for prayer is Saturday at 8:00 p.m. and is attended by a large majority of the congregation. Regular attendance signifies commitment to the work and is expected of those in places of ministry to the congregation.

Corporate prayer is also an integral part of our Tuesday evening home fellowship meetings and Friday night youth fellowship. These smaller groups afford an intimate setting for concentration on more specific prayer needs.

Half-nights of prayer, from 9:00 p.m. to 2:00 a.m., occur on scheduled Friday nights.

Occasional prayer retreats begin on Friday at 7:00 p.m. and go through 7:00 p.m. Saturday. This variety of times maintains our emphasis on corporate prayer and allows us to alter our scheduling as the Lord leads.

THE PROPER ATTITUDE

There is an expected protocol when meeting with royalty. In prayer we meet with the King of Kings, who is higher than any earthly sovereign. Our corporate approach to the Lord in prayer should reflect the proper attitude.

Esther's words from the Scriptures, "If it please the king," vocalize the attitude acceptable as we come before the Potentate of the whole earth. "Thine is the Kingdom and the power and the glory" are words expressive of His mighty Lordship. The hallowing of His name and the acknowledging of His power are pivotal considerations in the prayer Jesus taught His disciples to pray.

This does not suggest a dignified stuffiness, but rather a heartfelt reverence and honor. I have taught our congregation to begin focusing on the Lord *before* they enter the prayer room. Joking, loud talking, and doing business distract the heart and mind from the purpose of seeking God. We have agreed to reserve elaborate greetings for other occasions and direct our affections and energies on things above.

Also, people may become so accustomed to visitations of the Spirit in prayer that they become casual or even light in their attitude. Extended conversations with one another during a prayer meeting dishonor the Lord and are disrespectful to those praying. We have provided large foyer areas in order to preserve the sanctuary and prayer room for seeking the Lord.

BEGINNING THE MEETING

We approach our prayer meetings with the understanding that we have come to wait on the Lord—not to wait for others to arrive. We begin praying and looking to the Lord as soon as we enter the room and find a seat. Waiting for people to arrive only encourages lateness. An attitude of prayer and seeking is immediately established, and precious time is not wasted in everyone getting "settled." The projection is that we have come to meet with God. Our appointment is with Him. Being late not only distracts others, it dishonors the King.

Our prayer meetings begin with a time of personal, prayerful release to God. As we abandon ourselves to the Spirit, we step from the natural realm into a corporate waiting on the Lord. We enter His gates with thanksgiving, asking for His guidance, edifying ourselves in the Spirit. We cannot "conjure up" the flow of the Spirit, but we can quickly make ourselves available to His leading.

This is not a time to settle down in silence, but to stir up the gift of the Holy Spirit. We encourage people to pray aloud, not trying to overpower one another, but to give the fruit of their lips to God. Bible reading or silent meditation cannot substitute for releasing ourselves in prayer.

We have found a kneeling posture an aid to focusing our concentration on the Lord at the beginning of prayer meetings. Most members kneel at their chairs, or if they desire, stand or walk in worshiping the Lord behind those kneeling. The point is not the outward form but the inward motivation.

GATHERING THE PEOPLE

Usually our time of waiting on the Lord is focused by several members praying prayers of thanksgiving or requesting the Holy Spirit's guidance. Songs of the same nature allow a corporate voicing of our desires. Our identity as a body moving in prayer is established.

DIRECTION

As mentioned earlier, someone flowing in the spirit of prayer sets a direction for the meeting. This responsibility falls ultimately to the leader if no one else is exercised in this way. (The leader should not let a number of "dead" or scattered prayers at the beginning lower the level of unction to pray.)

Though a leader may never even pray aloud in a meeting, his presence sets the people free to flow with the Spirit. They know someone is taking the oversight of keeping order and balance and of ending the prayer meeting at the appropriate time.

When there is a good level of the spirit of prayer, prayers come one after another. People should lift their voices to be heard in order for the others to voice their agreement. If perhaps a child is having difficulty being heard beginning a prayer, an adult may say, "I make space for Billy to pray." We must be sensitive not to pray "on top of" the prayers of others.

When one flow or direction of prayer ends, sometimes there is a space of time before another begins. These spaces are not empty times but vital opportunities to receive the Spirit's direction. All should continue in an attitude of actively seeking the Lord.

MOODS OF THE SPIRIT

We do not draw hard lines of demarcation between prayer, praise, worship, prophecy, exhortation, or other expressions of God's presence among His people. Gathering for prayer is simply making ourselves, as a body, available to the Spirit of God. Our prayer meetings often include seasons of praise and worship; there is a piano in our prayer room to support these times. Times of repentance may find the entire gathering prostrate before the Lord, pouring out their hearts with much weeping. At certain times we are led to lay hands on individuals or certain groups (for example, musicians) within the gathering. There is room for prophecy and the song of the Lord when the level of anointing is appropriate. Members may even rise to give exhortations or share a Scripture. Praying the Scriptures is excellent; prefacing a prayer with a brief portion of Scripture strengthens our faith and brings the power of God's Word to bear in our praying.

The key lies in maintaining the focus of praying through the purposes of God. Meetings should not become songfests or teaching sessions. It is the responsibility of the prayer leaders to insure a liberty of the Spirit while preserving the integrity of the meeting.

DISCIPLINE OF CORPORATE PRAYER

Limitations of time prohibit many prayers from one single person. An individual should adjust the number of times he prays to the size of the gathering.

Corporate prayer demands a disciplined expression. We cannot pray whatever wanders into our mind—or sometimes even what is burning in our hearts—if it does not contribute to the flow set by the Spirit. Our prayers are directed to God but should allow others to agree and participate in their content. Rambling, mumbling, disconnected prayers show a lack of care for the corporate expression.

At the same time, the prayer meeting should exude a sense of family covering and love that allows the "least of these" to bring his offering and even be free to stumble and fall. *The only way to completely fail in prayer is to fail to pray!* The Lord looks on the heart. There is no greater eloquence than a prayer of sincerity and faith.

Voiced agreement is very much a part of the corporate expression in prayer. Though we pray aloud one at a time, our prayer thrust remains corporate. Though not overpowering, our agreement with the one praying should be obvious. Encouraging expressions such as "Yes, Lord! I agree with that prayer," uttered in sincerity, stir the level of faith to receive answers from the Lord. The Spirit's moving may solicit a reverential silence before the Lord, but the silence engendered by our flesh is simply deadness.

Our agreement is also expressed through our postures in a prayer meeting—standing, kneeling, clapping our hands, shouting, singing. As we give ourselves to the flow of the Spirit, the Lord is able to set His Church as an army in battle array. Unity (not uniformity) in expressions empowers the praying church.

CHILDREN

When God came to us in revival, He gave us this word of instruction: "Gather the people, sanctify the congregation, assemble the elders, gather the children, and those that suck the breast . . ." (Joel 2:16).

From that time it was clear to us that we were to include *all* of our children in the prayer meetings. Even infants and very small children quickly learned to remain quiet, sometimes sleep, or if old enough to talk, to enter into the praying and singing. We found that children are content if they are taught to participate in spiritual meetings.

We experienced a short period of distraction while parents were training their children, but the Holy Spirit arrested their young hearts and they soon became an integral part of the meetings. Parents and friends share the responsibility of holding or supervising young children during prayer meetings. It's a precious sight to see a father walking back and forth with his infant, tears streaming down his face in prayer.

Our children from speaking age (two to three) know that their prayers are welcomed in the corporate meetings. Their prayer vocabulary is developed considerably beyond their years. This would not be the case had they been relegated to another place while the adults prayed.

Some of our children have never known anything but revival and subsequent prayer meetings. One little fellow so esteemed the nights for prayer and church meetings that he termed evenings in between "nothing nights." As a result of this exposure and acceptance in prayer meetings, our children are exceptionally free in both prayer and worship. Some of them prophesy and sing the song of the Lord. It is not at all unusual for one or more of them to pray for me and other leaders before we preach or minister in worship services. A capacity to give themselves in prayer was developed in prayer meetings. We "suffered the little children," not forbidding them to come to

Jesus, and as we took their prayers seriously, they became pray-ers.

ENDING THE MEETING

The security of sensitive, responsible leadership again plays a vital role in drawing the meeting to an appropriate close. The larger the gathering, the more essential a definite closing becomes. Extending the meeting beyond the level of anointing and spiritual unction is just as damaging as cutting it off prematurely. We must avoid "wearing people out" in needlessly protracted meetings. All must be sensitive and not press to "get his prayer in." A closing song or appropriate closing prayer can be offered by one in leadership. It is good to end the meetings on an uplifting note. The exception to an "Amen" ending would be occasioned by a deep move of repentance where those still seeking the Lord would be left undisturbed while others would be released to leave as led. (The subject of leadership is further discussed in Part Five.)

CONCLUSION

In 1872, Henry Ward Beecher released for publication a series of lectures which he was asked to present to the Theological Department of Yale College. His series included one of the rare works in print on the subject of prayer meetings. Concerning meetings for prayer in general, he stated that "the prayer meeting is the voice of the church and of all its members." In mentioning some of the advantages of the church prayer meeting, Beecher observed that prayer meetings developed fellowship, discouraged a censorious spirit, cherished mutual helpfulness, discovered mutual needs, developed power in the congregation, and disclosed gifts and graces. He regarded it as the very heart and center of church life.[1]

The prayer meeting affords a regular, informal opportunity for individual members of the body to express the life of Christ being lived out through them. As Beecher describes it:

Here are the joys, the sorrows, the upliftings, the downcastings, all the ten thousand things which not only teach us to pray, but which pray in us and through us, with groanings that cannot be uttered. Is there any voice for these things, except as we gather up here and there a scrap from the congregation and make it known? Now, the ideal prayer is the voice of the Church, telling what it has learned of God in its daily conflict, bringing out the whole of the great range of Christian work that is going on in any community where there is a true church of Christ.[2]

The greatest blessing will result when care is taken to preserve the corporateness of the meeting. This takes specific effort, since it is easier for people to operate as individuals rather than to relate to the whole or to become spectators of the prayer performances of a few. We must teach the people to consider the best interest and purpose of the prayer meeting above their own personal desires or needs. This is a maturing process. Individuals will learn to defer to each other, but at the same time they need to learn that they must assume their portion of the responsibility to lead in prayer.

When flowing in a framework of liberty and love, the corporate prayer meeting is perhaps the most overt demonstration of the "body" reality of the church.

Notes

1. Henry Ward Beecher, *Yale Lectures on Preaching* (New York: Fords, Howard, and Hulbert, 1893), p. 57.
2. Ibid.

Part Three

Making the
Connection

Making the Connection

Introduction

Prayer is the believer's lifeline to the Father. It is the channel of our communion, the source of our direction, and the basis of our relationship with God. When we translate this concept to the corporate prayer life of the church, we begin to see the great significance of the church's prayer ministry. Prayer is the church's spiritual barometer. Prayer opens the windows of heaven, creating that certain atmosphere of liberty in which we receive the unction of God to build His Kingdom on earth.

The power is not simply in the act of gathering for prayer. The combining of each individual's personal communion with the Lord produces a corporate contact with the Godhead. This is the connection that infuses our Kingdom activities with eternal impact.

Prayer is the ingredient that makes the kingdoms of this world the kingdoms of our God. The Holy Spirit is not a "capricious influence" swooshing down on unsuspecting souls. As the arm of God in the earth, the Holy Spirit inhabits the hearts of the redeemed. His voice is prayer. He equips us to be ministers of reconciliation to a lost world. To God, the Spirit through us cries, "Abba, Father." The saints are edified by our releasing of the Spirit from within.

Our impact on the world and the vitality of our associations with the Father and fellow believers depend upon the prayer connection—prayer and outreach to the world, worship to the Lord, and revival to the Church.

10

Going Over the Wall

Outreach and Corporate Prayer

Successful endeavors are always launched from a platform of prayer. Through communion with the Lord in prayer, we receive direction for our outreach efforts. But prayer holds a broader significance concerning the expansion of our ministries beyond discerning what we are to do.

Prevenient Prayer

Paul declared, "For a great door and effectual is opened unto me, and there are many adversaries" (I Corinthians 16:9). Opportunities and adversaries come in the same package! Love and forgiveness are not everything. There is also a time to pray, "Avenge me of mine adversary" (Luke 18:3).

Daniel's visit to the lions' den illustrates this point. Disregarding the threats and pressures of those around him, Daniel continued to pray three times a day (Daniel 6:10). He was preparing himself, covering his ministry in prayer, to face a great crisis. In the place of prayer he put on the "whole armor of God" detailed in Ephesians 6:13-18—a description that ends with the admonition "praying always with all prayer and supplication in the Spirit, and watching thereunto with all perseverance and supplication for all the saints."

Daniel knew how to pray a prayer that would sustain him in the lions' den. This is the prayer of *prevenience*—that is, praying *ahead* of the devil. So often we launch our projects, enter a crisis, and then pray in alarm when things begin to go wrong. The church that succeeds in its mission is the one that prays in advance of its mission.

Jesus included prevenient prayer in His model for His disciples: "And lead us not into temptation, but deliver us from evil" (Matthew 6:13). With the awareness that there will be temptations and evil, we fortify ourselves through the prayer that will go ahead to prepare the way.

It is not enough to receive the Father's plan for outreach in our ministries. To insure the success of the particular mission we are given, we must continually safeguard our efforts through prevenient praying. The lions we face as we seek to win the world for Christ have the same potential for damage as Daniel's "den-mates." "Be sober, be vigilant; because your adversary the devil, as a roaring lion, walketh about, seeking whom he may devour: Whom resist steadfast in the faith . . ." (I Peter 5:8,9).

We are called to be more than defenders of the faith—we are to be contenders for the faith of Christ in the earth. Praying ahead of our exploits for God allows us to command an offensive position against our adversary.

Prevenient praying precludes presumption by "covering all the bases." It arms us in a general sense (Daniel prepared for whatever consequences he would have to suffer). It also teaches us to pray specifically. For example, before I go out to minister in a particular situation, our congregation seeks to saturate the effort with prayer, from my plane reservations to the Word I will minister. The Lord has taught us to pray for our prayers, that we may discern the wiles of the devil and thwart his schemes beforehand in prayer.

Prevenient prayer in the corporate setting assumes a special significance. The Scriptures often speak of the church as the army of God. God's plan is for His army to establish His Kingdom on earth. Lone warriors, however gifted, will never accomplish His purposes. In corporate prayer, every member of the body assembles on the front lines of the outreach effort. The responsibility of the effort—and the rewards of the victory—are equally shared. As we put the devil on the defensive, the gates of hell shall not prevail against the prayers of the church.

Beyond the prayer of prevenience, there is a realm of spiritual authority that maintains open doors in given areas of outreach. This offensive measure also finds its impetus in corporate prayer.

GAINED GROUND

The testimony of Rees Howells, the renowned intercessor and leader of a powerful corporate prayer gathering, introduced me to the concept of "gained ground" in prayer. Once we pray through to a place of attainment in the spiritual realm, we can maintain ministries in that realm through prevailing prayer. It appears the enemy must yield up certain strongholds once we bring them down in prayer. S. D. Gordon has said it this way: "The enemy yields only what he must. He yields only what is taken. Therefore the ground must be taken step by step."[1]

Satan intimidates as a pretender prince. Though he walks about *as* a roaring lion, he *was* defeated at Calvary. The purpose of our prayers is to enforce the victory of Calvary through faith.

At times our efforts to reach out with the claims of the Gospel appear to be stymied. Again, Gordon sheds light on the necessity of "praying it through" before we attempt to "make it true": "Prayer is striking the winning blow at the concealed enemy. Service is gathering up the results of that blow among the men we see and touch."[2]

Gaining ground necessitates a spiritual maturing and expansion in the realm of corporate prayer. Our own experience at Shekinah illustrates the process. In the several years following the 1980 visitation of the Lord that established the corporate prayer ministry of our church, our local sphere of ministry expanded in scope and depth. Our annual conferences and Shekinah Bible Institute, in particular, increased rapidly in size, drawing ministers from around the world for inspiration and training. Other ministries to area prisons, nursing homes, and various musical and evangelistic outreaches flourished. All these efforts were supported by a consistent corporate prayer life.

But in 1984 we stepped out of our local area to establish an extension of our Bible school in India and a branch church in another state. Though we had engaged in international ministry for some years, these efforts would sink roots into yet unclaimed areas. We soon learned that while both of these ventures were in the will of God for us, the enemy was not going to surrender his territory without a fight.

While we were in India laying the foundations for the Bible school, one of the men in our congregation had a vivid dream that an enemy called "The Destroyer" was at work against Shekinah.

At the time we did not discern the significance of this warning. But upon my return from India, I realized the enemy had begun to work through a few people in backbiting and deceitful thoughts. Jealousies and other disharmonies arose in certain areas. Then the Lord led us to discover this interesting fact: "The Destroyer" is the name of one of the Hindu gods of India! It seemed that he had mounted a retaliation against the work that was going to tear down his kingdom there.

So the Lord said to me, "You'd better get your praying shoes on and before you take any more territory, find out how to take it first in prayer. Pray there before you go there." The Lord gave us understanding about varying realms of outreach from the Scripture in Genesis 49:22,23:

Joseph is a fruitful bough, even a fruitful

bough by a well; whose branches run over the wall: the archers have sorely grieved him, and shot at him, and hated him.

He showed us that the devil has a different response to outreach in "outside the wall" territory. Our corporate prayer ministry had to mature to pray through our expansions.

In 1985 we began a building expansion. The Lord told us, "Now I'm changing the sacrifice." We understood, from the book of Leviticus, that the Lord prescribed what the order of the sacrifice would be. The Lord spoke to me, "I have the right to change the order of your sacrifice of prayer. I want you to pray corporately *every morning*." We immediately began 6:00 a.m. prayer meetings (7:00 a.m. on weekends).

The fresh impetus we received from obeying this direction has been astounding. We came to understand that we had stepped out in ministry in advance of our praying, and this new sacrifice would allow us to "catch up." A freshness and life has entered our corporate praying, accompanied by an assurance that we have gained the ground in prayer for other efforts in the realm of extension schools and branch churches. We need only pray about which doors we should enter, for the territory has been taken and is maintained in prayer.

If God has not dealt with the enemy's strongholds in an area, we will never be a match for their power. But if we send our prayers before us and obey the Lord's "order of sacrifice," we have gained the ground before we arrive there in the natural realm. Then our outreach will be a true Kingdom gain, because when God opens doors, no man can close them.

FOUNDATION GROUND OF REVELATION AND FAITH

Gained ground in outreach ministry must be based on a foundation laid through revelation and faith. These spiritual elements comprise the platform from which to launch our expansions "over the wall."

As in the natural realm, the Lord begins the building of His foundation with a period of *excavation*. When God first came to us in revival, He dealt with sins of unforgiveness, ambition, jealousy, and irreconciliation until He united the body to pray in agreeing faith. He then began to give us a revelation of Himself and His work on the cross. He gave us a depth of understanding of brokenness and repentance in order for us to know these must be a way of life. He then dealt meticulously by subject with such sins in the church as pride, anger, intemperance, and sins of the tongue.

His work was exacting and thorough. Each step of dealing became an Ebenezer: "Hitherto hath the Lord helped us" (I Samuel 7:12). We knew that God had brought us there for His purpose. The enemy could not make us doubt the revelation we had of ourselves and our God. So the places were ours. They were gained ground.

After the period of excavation, the Lord began to lay a foundation of faith—all of this in meetings for prayer. Day after day our faith was strengthened by revelation from His Word: the working of grace, the power of His love, the work of the Spirit, the reality of healing, and countless others.

The treasures the Lord gave us by His Spirit became as real to us as tangible objects. He taught them, and since we have experienced them for ourselves they cannot be questioned; they are gained ground.

ASKING FOR NATIONS

After establishing us on a foundation of revelation and faith, God revealed Himself to us as the Lord of the Harvest.

> Then saith he unto his disciples, The harvest truly is plentious, but the labourers are few; Pray ye therefore the Lord of the harvest, that he will send forth labourers into his harvest (Matthew 9:37-38).

The perimeters of our vision were broadened to embrace the whole world; our faith was expanded to ask largely of the Lord for a plenteous harvest in the nations of the earth. In a new sense, we became world Christians.

The impact of our praying the Lord of the Harvest involved our willingness to be the laborers we prayed for, and indeed, we have sent a number of workers to the nations of the earth. Having gained the ground in prayer, we are able to sink spiritual roots into other nations through Bible schools and training of foreign leaders in our local Bible college. Missions is no longer a jungle to us, for the Lord of the Harvest has charted a path for us to follow. The doors to the nations are open.

Now it is not unusual for a prayer meeting or worship service to have an emphasis for one or more nations. Strongholds are brought down in invisible realms through prayer and worship. Once taken in prayer, these areas become spiritually gained ground. Having struck the winning blow at the concealed enemy through prayer, we or others can go into that territory and reap the harvest of the Lord.

Notes

1. S. D. Gordon, Quiet Talks on Prayer (New York: Grosset & Dunlap, 1941), p. 36.
2. Ibid., p. 21.

11

The Father Seeketh Such

Worship and Corporate Prayer

Throughout the Scriptures, expressions of prayer and worship continually appear together. The Psalms exhibit a free-flowing mixture of praise, rejoicing, prayer to God, and worship of Him. In the New Testament, those who made requests of Jesus often came worshiping Him. More specifically, Paul mentioned both prayer and expressions of worship as integral elements in the assemblies of the saints. Our understanding of the connection between these two will materially effect the depth of our experience in corporate worship.

RESTORATION OF WORSHIP

Since the nadir of the church in the Dark Ages, God has progressively restored revelation of His truth to His body in the earth. Following the Reformation which brought the Church back to salvation by faith, the truth of sanctification was restored through the Wesleys and others. Others built on these doctrines, and with the recovering of the baptism of the Holy Spirit with His gifts at the turn of this century, the 1900s have witnessed a restoration of the five-fold ministry (Ephesians 4:11) and God's order for His Church.

We are living in the days when worship is being revitalized in the Church. Jesus promised that there would come a day when true worshipers would worship the Father in Spirit and in truth:

> But the hour cometh, and now is, when the true worshipers shall worship the Father in spirit and in truth: for the Father seeketh such to worship him (John 4:23).

The preaching of God's Word is no less precious. The great commission to make disciples must continually be fulfilled. But none of the works that we do for God can ever satisfy the longing of our souls and His own desire that we worship Him in spirit and truth. Churches around the world are discovering this fact and are setting about to bring true worship into their weekly services. Now it is not unusual for churches to spend an hour singing, praising, even dancing or bowing before the Lord, enjoying His presence. Such congregations are not going through motions or following a schedule but are spontaneously expressing an offering of their whole hearts to God.

Many churches have entered into the New Testament reality of corporate worship:

> Speaking to yourselves in psalms and hymns and spiritual songs, singing and making melody in your heart to the Lord (Ephesians 5:19).

> Let the word of Christ dwell in you richly in all wisdom; teaching and admonishing one another in psalms and hymns and spiritual songs, singing with grace in your hearts to the Lord (Colossians 3:16).

> . . . when ye come together, every one of you hath a psalm, hath a doctrine, hath a tongue, hath a revelation, hath an interpretation. Let all things be done unto edifying (I Corinthians 14:26).

Many enjoy free praise, the song of the Lord, and a prophetic flow. In services where there is a good level of anointing for these expressions, there will be conviction of sin and repentance, miracles of healing and deliverance, and revelation as the presence of God draws near.

COMMUNION: THE BASIS OF WORSHIP

To those who desire true worship, it becomes apparent that some churches experience a higher level of worship than do others. A greater reality, more liberty, a keener sense of God's presence is evident. Personal needs are met in the assembly of worshipers.

The obvious response of the inquiring heart is "Why? What makes the difference? What are the factors involved?" Often churches endeavor to duplicate or mimic the forms of worship they admire. Perhaps they build an orchestra, hire a music minister, change the order of the service, imitate postures, or use different songs.

I appreciate the need to teach certain procedures and techniques to facilitate the worship service. To this end, our church hosts an annual worship conference and sends worship teams to assist other churches. Excellence is desirable. A pleasing sound is very helpful. Understanding Scriptures relating to worship is necessary. But worship itself is none of these.

We can be lulled into thinking that worship really is music, spontaneity, a free-flowing service. Worship is not music. Music is a *vehicle* for worship. Worship is not *any* particular form. A worshiping church is not a church that incorporates worship expressions.

A worshiping church is a collection of worshiping hearts gathered to be poured out before their God. The Lord once gave me this little statement: To have a worshiping church, you must have worshipers. That may sound too simple, but unless there are worshiping hearts, there will not be true worship—only worship mechanics. A worshiping church must be made up of worshipers, not merely of believers who have come to a "worship" service.

Worshipers are people who have relationships of communion with the Lord. They have been with Jesus because they are pray-ers. True worship comes from a relationship of love to the Father. Prayer expresses that relationship. Prayer is communion and devotion. It opens the way to repentance which keeps our relationship with God vital. This vitality then comes forth in our worship.

No one can hand us a formula for producing true worship. Worship is developed in prayer. *Those churches who worship in Spirit and truth are praying churches.* The level of worship will be directly commensurate with the level of prayer. To attempt to separate worship from a prayer life is to take the warmth and light from the flame.

PRE-SERVICE PRAYER

Orchestral and vocal practices are an understood necessity, but preparation of the spiritual atmosphere is the determining factor relating to God's presence and true worship. The techniques and music itself can be marvelous, but those can be bought from the world. The essential life of God is received only in communion with Him. Preparation for a worship service is done in prayer. Pre-service prayer affords a time of *immediate* preparation to focus on the Lord, to stand on spiritual tiptoe and enter into communion with His Spirit.

We have maintained pre-service prayer as a standard from the beginning days of our church. For thirty minutes prior to the appointed time of the service, the whole congregation gathers in the sanctuary to seek God and settle their hearts in preparation for worship. We have found that more is accomplished if this time is given specifically to praying, rather than singing to the Lord, which will occur in the worship service to follow.

Some musicians and worship leaders may spend a few minutes privately praying for each other. Others, especially the children, often come and pray for me or other ministers. But the focus of this time is releasing our faith *to the Lord* for His presence among us. We do this both as individuals (for instance, at the beginning of a prayer meeting), and corporately, as one may read a Scripture aloud or lift his voice to lead in prayer. Expressions of praise are appropriate if there is a "deadness." Pre-service prayer is a special time of shaking off the "dust" of our daily living and preparing our spirit-man to meet with our Beloved, the King.

Reserving this time for prayer is a discipline, as there is a temptation to greet and fellowship with one another at this time. Fellowship is wonderful; it just doesn't have any power to prepare the spiritual atmosphere for the worship service. Given that there will be time to fellowship after the service, we can discipline ourselves and agree together to use the pre-service prayer time wisely.

Pre-service prayer will not happen unless it is taught, and it will not continue unless the pastor insists upon it and is himself an example. All who minister in our orchestra or lead worship are required to attend pre-service prayer. If they feel this is more than they can do, we release them from responsibility in music ministry.

Some churches feel that they just cannot function musically without a certain person and choose to compromise a standard to accommodate that person. As a result, they may have better music, but they will have less preparation for the experience of true worship. This usually translates into less reality and a lack of the presence of God.

Unfortunately, a casual attitude toward pre-service prayer is very common. An indifference to preparing oneself for the services indicates a "spectator mentality." Too often believers come to church to see what "they"—the worship leaders, pastor, musicians—are going to do. They come to join in the worship forms of singing, clapping, or dancing. But they fail to grasp the *purpose* of worship: to pour out the heart before the Lord.

Our desire to worship must be matched with an understanding of the intention of the truly worshiping heart. Then we can appreciate the place of prayer and honor it as the entrance to worship.

12

If My People Will . . . Pray

Revival and Corporate Prayer

Now when Solomon had made an end of praying, the fire came down from heaven, and consumed the burnt offering and the sacrifice; and the glory of the Lord filled the house (II Chronicles 7:1).

Revival is a supernatural fire. The pattern of prayer and revival seen in this verse is God's way of bringing His visitation among His people. Solomon finished praying; then the fire came down and the glory filled the house.

Likewise in Acts 2, after the 120 had prayed and waited on God, the fire fell and a sound as a rushing mighty wind was sent from above. When heavenly sounds are dying out, it is because prayer is dying out.

The two elements that work together to bring and maintain revival are prayer and repentance—always. Sometimes men have spent weeks and months in prayer for revival, perhaps meeting together on a set day each week. But unless there comes a work of repentance in their hearts, they are not prepared for revival.

God's way for revival is delineated in II Chronicles 7:14:

> If my people, which are called by my name, shall humble themselves, and pray, and seek my face, and turn from their wicked ways; then will I hear from heaven, and will forgive their sin, and will heal their land.

THE PRINCIPLE

II Chronicles 7:14 is the embodiment of the complete revival principle. The key words are these:

1) My people—Revival begins with God's people praying.

2) Humble themselves—It is humbling to pray. Pride conceals our great need. The humility of changing our lifestyles in order to pray reveals the desperateness of our need.

3) Pray—Actually pour out our hearts before God. He is waiting for us to ask Him.

4) Seek my face—This is not only praying but waiting on God, listening for His voice. "He is a rewarder of those who diligently seek Him (Hebrews 11:6). Seeking definitely implies an extended searching.

5) Turn from wicked ways—Repentance is experienced as we humble ourselves in prayer. The Holy Spirit convicts the heart which presents itself in humility.

THE PERSON

An old revivalist stood in our sanctuary one day, and seeing my yearning for revival and the presence of God, he said to me softly, "If you can get *Him* to come. . . ." I found that this is what revival is. Revival is not an it. Revival is a person—the Holy Spirit. "When he is come, He will reprove the world of sin, and of righteousness, and of judgment" (John 16:8). He is God's agent for revival.

THE PREPARATION

He comes to a people prepared for Him. He will be grieved and go away if provision is not made for His welcome through prayer and repentance. It has been said of the Welsh people that they possessed "the wail of a soul"—a continuous cry for revival. They placed religious pursuits above all else.

John the Baptist came crying, "Prepare ye the way of the Lord" (Matthew 3:3). He was fulfilling the prophecy of Isaiah 40:3-8. This Scripture completes the picture of preparation. It is a work of humbling and repentance that can come only through prayer.

In 1985 I went to minister in New Zealand for the first time. The Lord wondrously met us in melting and repentance. His presence brought a wonderful unity between many of the leaders present at the meetings. I sent a telegram home to Shekinah. It read, "He came." The people at home knew exactly what that meant. The people in New Zealand had prepared the way of the Lord through prayer. They were ready to repent. The Holy Spirit was welcomed through their preparation. Experientially and historically speaking, God has come in revival in answer to prayer.

The Preservation

In our own experience, we found that revival was preserved and extended through prayer. The congregation prayed night and day for twelve weeks, and then continued in the strength of that visitation for several years. It brought vitality and unity, and gave us strength to birth outreach ministries and believe God for the impossible.

Prayer was the bellows that blew upon the warm coals of revival and kept the body glowing with fervency. The leadership prayed before and after the corporate prayer meetings—we prayed beforehand for the prayer meetings, and afterward to seal the work of the Spirit.

In the prayer meetings themselves, the Holy Spirit would daily teach us to pray. He would pray through us. He would convict us of sin, and we would repent. He would reveal truths from the Word, and we would rejoice or weep. He is a praying Spirit.

THE PRODUCT

Revival historians call the year 1858-1859 the Annus Mirabulus—Year of Miracles. The countries of Japan, China, and India all opened to the Gospel through treaties with Great Britain. This was the great revival that spawned men, movements, and missions as never before. Dwight Moody, Andrew Murray, and William Booth received their great impetus at this time. The Salvation Army was born, and Hudson Taylor's China Inland Mission reported an increase in conversions of 25 percent.

It began with one man who called a few other businessmen together for prayer on their lunch hour in New York. Within six months ten thousand or more men in New York City alone were praying at the noon hour. A traveling man mentioned that he found a prayer meeting that extended from Omaha to New York.

Another Wave Rolls In, written by Frank Bartleman, gives a studied account of the prayer effort which made the way for the Azusa Street Revival at the turn of the century. Bartleman kept in touch with Evan Roberts, who was leading revival in Wales at that time. They prayed corporately, both to prepare the way and to continue the move of revival. In America and Wales, hearts were bound in agreeing faith. That fire soon had burned its way around the world. It began with a few men praying.

For God to bring revival, He must come to hearts that are prepared (Malachi 3:1). We put ourselves in the place of preparation through prayer. The Holy Spirit then does the work that brings cleansing and repentance. A revived people can thus pray for a revival movement. "If my people . . . will pray. . . ." Prayer prepares the heart for revival, and only continuing in prayer can preserve the revival. Prayer is to revival as fuel is to the flame.

Part Four

Incentives to Prayer

Incentives to Prayer

Introduction

Jesus declared, "It is written, My house shall be called the house of prayer" (Matthew 21:13; cf. Isaiah 56:7). Prayer is *the business of the Father's house.* Because of its pivotal position in the life of the Kingdom, prayer is a main target in the enemy's assaults against the Church. The devil seeks to cripple our prayer efforts by robbing us of the incentives the Lord has provided to motivate us to pray. The enemy's goal is to tear down our expectations from God—to undermine our faith.

Even churches long established in the framework of corporate prayer must guard against satan's subtle devices. If the enemy cannot prevent us from praying, he will attempt to rob our prayers of their power, consequently discouraging us through our failure to receive answers. Faith is the power of prayer, for "without faith it is impossible to please God" (Hebrews 11:6). Faith is the essential ingredient to answered prayer. "And all things, whatsoever ye shall ask in prayer, *believing*, ye shall receive" (Matthew 21:22, emphasis added). Harold Horton said, "Faith is the normal atmosphere of heaven, so difficult to acquire on earth because all hell is against it."[1]

The enemy's weapon against our power in prayer is unbelief. The devil seeks to engulf our perception of God and His ways in clouds of doubt. This fog of unbelief often arises from our own entrenched misconceptions and false assumptions concerning the will of God and His response to His children.

I have observed that there is a kind of *community unbelief* that can strangle our efforts in corporate prayer. In His own country Jesus did not do many mighty works because of the community unbelief (Matthew 13:58). He denounced entire cities because they refused to repent and believe. God has obligated Himself to work with and through our faith. Therefore unbelief is not merely a failure; it is an absolute tragedy. It can keep churches from moving in the plan of God.

The principle of agreement becomes negatively powerful when a group of people gathered for prayer is ensnared by unbelief. The enemy's web of deception tricks us into being content in offering faithless prayers. Unless a voice arises to bring a disclaimer against such postures of unbelief, the whole prayer effort may become trapped in these comfortable assumptions.

There are three particular areas of doubt concerning the character and ways of God in relation to prayer. These challenges to our faith appear in the following questions:

1) Is God willing to answer our prayers?
2) Will God hear our prayers?
3) Do our prayers matter to God?

Clearing away these three clouds of unbelief will thwart the enemy's devices and establish our churches as true houses of prayer.

Note

1. Quoted in Judson Cornwall, *Unfeigned Faith* (Old Tappan, New Jersey: Fleming H. Revell Company), p. 22.

13

An Unwilling God is Not the Problem

An Attitude of Confidence in Corporate Prayer

In that day you will no longer ask me anything. I tell you the truth, my Father will give you whatever you ask in my name. Until now you have not asked for anything in my name. Ask and you will receive, and your joy will be complete (John 16:23-24, NIV).

In commenting on this passage, S. D. Gordon has noted that the original Greek of verse 24 is much stronger than the usual renderings. He contends that the understanding is "Ask; I ask you to ask." Obviously, God has ordained that we ask of Him. His expressed attitude is that of great desire. However we perceive this injunction—as an invitation, a request, or a command—we must be equally assured of God's simultaneous promise ". . . and you *will* receive."

As Christians, we have a contract with a God who cannot lie. His implicit intention is that we not only ask but that we receive whatever we desire of Him. Often our response to an unsatisfied expectation is to *question God's willingness to answer our prayers*. Our perception of His intention becomes clouded. In our unbelief, we pretend that Jesus did not really say His Father wanted to answer all of our requests. To stand in the place of faith, we must be convinced of God's true motives in desiring to answer us.

Our Joy, His Glory

God's motives in answering our prayers are so preciously pure that we often stumble at them. The Lord intends that answered prayer make us happy, so that "your joy will be complete." Why? Verse 27 of the same chapter in John says, ". . . the Father Himself loves you." God demonstrates His love by giving: "For God so loved the world that He gave . . ." (John 3:16). Answering our prayers is a fundamental part of the Father's confirmation of love and acceptance of His children. Answered prayer demonstrates the love relationship between the church and God the Father.

John 15:7-8 gives further insight into the purpose of answered prayer:

If you remain in me and my words remain in you, ask whatever you wish, and it will be given you. This is to my Father's glory, that you bear much fruit, showing yourselves to be my disciples (NIV).

Beyond blessing us with joy, receiving answers to prayer *glorifies God!* Asking and receiving is not shallow or carnal. Sometimes we labor in a false notion of piety that prayer is an end in itself. That's not faith—that's floundering. God's purpose is for us to continue in prayer. Keep on asking and keep on receiving, that His name might be glorified.

AN ATTITUDE OF ASKING

We can then view prayer as part of our labor "together with God." Asking and receiving expresses our union with the Father.

Assurance that the Lord expects us to ask and desires to answer enables us to come to Him in confidence. The following three elements should constitute our "attitude of asking":

1) Know that God *expects* you to ask.
2) Know that He *desires* to give and complete your joy.
3) Come *confidently* to Him in prayer.

Prayer is designed to work for us, not against

us. Any struggle we encounter in prayer is against our own flesh or against the devil. We don't wrestle with God. The angel came to wrestle against Jacob's flesh to enable him to walk with God in faith (Genesis 32:24-30).

The answer to Daniel's prayers was delayed by the devil under the guise of the Prince of Persia; God was willing to answer from the first day Daniel prayed. *An unwilling God is not the problem.*

RIGHTLY DIVIDING THE WORD

Why have we thought we have to wrench from God's hand that which He has told us He will give us if we ask Him? Part of the answer lies in our difficulty in "rightly dividing the Word of truth," for "faith comes by hearing, and hearing by the word of God" (Romans 10:17). Failure to rightly divide the Word clouds our faith and even allows us to remain comfortable in our unbelief.

But as we rightly divide the Word, light will come upon Scriptures we have previously read with a bias. Two such Scriptures that relate to God's willingness to answer our prayers are the parable of the importunate man needing bread in Luke 11 and the parable of the unjust judge in Luke 18.

Somehow we have supposed that Jesus' emphasis in these parables was upon *persistence* in asking of the Lord, almost as though we had to wear down His resistance to our desires. In truth, the parable of the man needing bread at midnight is an understanding of God's *willingness* to give. In Luke 11, the Greek word translated "importunity" in verse 8 (KJV) does not mean persistence or repetition in asking, but rather suggests confidence: "I say unto you, though he will not rise and give him because he is his friend, yet because of his *importunity* he will rise and give him as many as he needeth." The word is **anaideia**, meaning "boldly; without shamefacedness." The point, then, is that God responds not to our repeated asking but to our *attitude of confidence*, of faith that He will hear us. This confidence comes from our understanding of the way and character of God.

In that light, it is the willing nature of our Heavenly Father that is portrayed in Luke 18. Jesus contrasts the unjust judge, who must be "worn down" through repeated requests, with God, the just Judge, who answers speedily.

A RELATIONSHIP OF TRUST

Our ultimate answer to the cloud of "Is God willing to answer our prayers?" is found in Luke 11:

Which of you fathers, if your son asks for a fish, will give him a snake instead? Or if he asks for an egg, will give him a scorpion? If you then, though you are evil, know how to give good gifts to your children, how much more will your Father in heaven give the Holy Spirit to those who ask Him! (verses 11-13, NIV).

To ask in boldness, we must know the relationship we have with the Father. Our faith is based in the trust we have in the character of God as our Father in heaven. The key to confidence in the relationship of asking is truly believing "I'm asking my Father."

We must throw off our "poverty mentality" concerning our Father. He is the God of the fatted calf! What the prodigal in Luke 15 received certainly wasn't a reward for his persistence in prayer, for he didn't even get to voice his request! The Father lavishly gave to the son because of who He (the Father) was. When we elevate our opinion of God as the loving Father, then we will expect Him to do wonderful things for His children. The cloud of doubt is dispelled.

14

Knowing He Hears Us

Assurance of Our Position in Corporate Prayer

And this is the confidence that we have in him, that, if we ask any thing according to his will, he heareth us: And if we know that he hear us, whatsoever we ask, we know that we have the petitions that we desired of him (I John 5:14,15).

A second cloud that moves in to defeat our prayer efforts is the question of the Lord *hearing* or giving audience to our asking. Again the key to dispelling the cloud is attaining a position of confidence concerning the ways and provisions of God.

Implied in the above Scripture is the understanding that it is one thing to ask of the Lord and another thing for Him to hear—that our asking and His hearing are not synonymous. The question of confidence arises in *knowing He hears* our prayers. How do we know He hears us?

The two pertinent factors found in this Scripture are the conditions of *asking according to His will* and *assurance that He has heard*. We must develop confidence in these areas. Probably the greatest deterrent to having this confidence is a lack of understanding in how we are to come before God's throne in prayer.

HOW TO COME BEFORE THE THRONE

The scriptural example of Queen Esther gives us a picture of the concept of "coming before the throne." The success of Esther's mission depended upon her being *heard* by the King.

> When he [the king] saw Queen Esther standing in the court, he was pleased with her and held out to her the gold scepter that was in his hand. So Esther approached and touched the tip of the scepter. Then the King asked, ... What is your request? (Esther 5:2,3)

Esther's acceptance into the king's presence was an unknown. It was a risk she took. The King of Kings wants so much to make His blessings available to us that He has made a supernatural provision giving us *unlimited* access to His throne of grace: This provision is the blood of Jesus.

The blood is the gift of God. We cannot enter His presence by acts of striving. Our confidence level can be no higher than our willingness to trust Him to do what He has promised. Every time we come to the place of prayer, we must approach God with the peaceful confidence that He has made a way for us that we can simply accept.

Certainly sin will keep our prayers from being heard. "If I regard iniquity in my heart, the Lord will not hear me" (Psalm 66:18). But the blood is God's remedy for sin. "If we confess our sins, he is faithful and just to forgive us our sins, and to cleanse us from all unrighteousness" (I John 1:9); ". . . and the blood of Jesus Christ his Son cleanseth us from all sin" (verse 7).

The requirement for cleansing is confession, not groveling. He forgives *immediately* and cleanses by Jesus' blood. Thus our access to the throne of a hearing God is instantaneously restored.

> Having therefore, brethren, boldness to enter into the holiest by the blood of Jesus, By a new and living way, which he hath consecrated for us, through the vail, that is to say, his flesh . . . Let us draw near with a true heart in full assurance of faith, having our hearts sprinkled from an evil conscience . . . (Hebrews 10:19,20,22).

The ploy of the enemy is to undermine our confidence through condemnation. The reality of continual access to God's throne through the blood of Jesus is our mighty weapon against this device of the devil.

Determining the Will of God

First John 5:14, clearly says that our confidence in being heard by God is contingent upon our asking *according to His will*. The enemy wants us to believe that we can never know the will of God. His plan is to cloud God's purposes and leave us wandering in a fog of confusion and discouragement.

But God has *asked* us to determine His will:

> For this cause we also . . . do not cease to pray for you, and to desire that ye might be filled with the knowledge of his will in all wisdom and understanding (Colossians 1:9).

> . . . that ye may stand perfect and complete in all the will of God (Colossians 4:12).

> And be not conformed to this world: but be ye transformed by the renewing of your mind, that ye may prove what is that good, and acceptable, and perfect, will of God (Romans 12:2).

God not only wants us to determine his will; He has made a second supernatural provision that we might *pray* His will in confidence. That provision is the Holy Spirit. Once we have confidence that we have entered by the cleansing power of Jesus' blood, we begin to operate in prayer through the Holy Spirit; that is, we allow the Holy Spirit to pray through us.

> Likewise the Spirit also helpeth our infirmities: for we know not what we should pray for as we ought: but the Spirit itself maketh intercession for us ... because he maketh intercession for the saints according to the will of God (Romans 8:26,27).

God has made a provision by His Spirit to make up our lack in knowing how to pray. Actually, God's intention is not so much that we should know how to pray as that we should *learn how to let the One who prays through us do His work.* The Holy Spirit knows the will of God and does not make mistakes in interceding for the saints. His prayers are *always* heard and answered. Releasing ourselves to the Spirit's intercession is not difficult, though it is supernatural. The Holy Spirit resides in every born again person, and He cries from within us to the Father (Romans 8:15, Galatians 4:6).

Through the blood of Jesus and the power of the Holy Spirit, the process of being heard of God and answered by Him is complete. Our access to the throne is perpetual through the blood of Jesus. The Holy Spirit resident in believers forms a prayer to the Father according to His will. That prayer comes through our lips. We have prayed; we know He hears us; and we have what we have asked.

In the process of prayer, we find the Persons of the Trinity working in concert to insure our success. Our work is not in striving, but in releasing; not in doing, but in allowing. It may be more "natural" to strive in our flesh, but we won't receive answers, which is the purpose for praying.

Prayer is a spiritual exercise. We must come to God in faith, applying the blood of Jesus to our sins and allowing the Holy Spirit to pray the will of God through us. Then there is no doubt that we are heard.

15

Believing Our Prayers Make the Difference

Responsibility and Privilege of Corporate Prayer

The final cloud of unbelief that shadows our faith can be the most damaging of all. Through it, the enemy seeks to cut the heart out of our prayers, leaving us with an impotent void. The crucial question is "Do our prayers really make a difference?"

Consider the following two opposing philosophies. John Wesley taught, "God does nothing except in answer to prayer." He established his ministry on this principle. The fatalist says, "What will be, will be." Convinced that prayer has no effect, he does not pray. Unfortunately, most people are in the mediocre middle (or muddle) between these two opinions. This is why most people either don't pray or pray with little conviction.

Great believing results in great praying. But

many Christians do not know what they believe about prayer. Believing what God's Word teaches will revolutionize our expectations in prayer. Discovering what God intends for His people to accomplish through prayer will convince us of our responsibility and privilege. It will blow away the cloud of "Does it matter?" and build the foundation of understanding that God's plan is to do His work on earth through the prayers of men.

BLOWING AWAY THE CLOUD

E. M. Bounds, in his book *The Reality of Prayer*, stated:

We have much fine writing and learned talk about the subjective benefits of prayer; how prayer secures its full measure of results, not by affecting God, but by affecting us, by becoming a training school for those who pray. We are taught by such teachers that the province of prayer is not to get, but to train. Prayer thus becomes a mere performance, a drill-sergeant, a school, in which patience, tranquility and dependence are taught. In this school, denial of prayer is the most valuable teacher. How well all this may look, and how reasonable soever it may seem, there is nothing of it in the Bible. The clear and oft-repeated language of the Bible is that prayer is to be answered by God; that God occupies the relation of a father to us, and that as Father, He gives to us when we ask the things for which we ask. The best praying, therefore, is the praying that gets an answer.

It sounds very spiritual to be willing to pray and not see answers. In reality, that is the main vapor in the "Does it matter?" cloud. How illusive, unpredictable, and uninspiring; also, how untrue!

We can make two clear statements on this issue:

1) The Lord *Himself* does not change. His character and nature are absolutely dependable (cf. Malachi 3:6).
2) He does change what He has said He will *do* under certain conditions—those conditions being prayer and repentance.

Abraham. In Genesis 18 the Lord told Abraham what He was obligated to do in order to uphold His own righteous character (which will not change). Abraham began to intercede in order to determine under what conditions God would spare the cities of Sodom and Gomorrah. His prayer ascertained God's minimum requirement to spare the city (verse 32). God was willing to change what He intended to do, but only under *certain conditions*.

Moses. In Exodus 32 the Israelites corrupted themselves by worshiping other gods. The Lord told Moses that He was planning to destroy them *if Moses would leave Him alone* (v.10). But Moses did not leave God alone. He presented arguments based on God's Word. He reminded God of His promises to Abraham to establish a people. He argued that the Egyptians would misunderstand God (verses 11-13). As a result, the Lord *repented* of the evil He thought to do against the people (verse 14).

On another occasion, when God threatened to smite the Israelites with a pestilence and disinherit them for their murmuring and rebellion (Numbers 14:12), Moses advanced some of the same arguments (verses 13-19). The Lord again pardoned their sin (verse 20). Intercession again altered the Lord's expressed intentions.

THE RESPONSIBILITY: STANDING IN THE GAP

God is both righteous and merciful. His righteousness requires that He bring judgment upon sin; His mercy desires a way to avoid it. In Ezekiel 22 God rehearsed all the evil deeds of the "bloody city." His justice promised destruction (verses 21-22). But His mercy "sought for a man among them, that should make up the hedge, and stand in the gap before me for the land, that I should not destroy it" (verse 30).

Unfortunately He could not find one. Therefore He poured out His indignation upon them (verse 31). If a man had stood in the gap, God could have righteously spared the city. That was the desire of His mercy.

A praying man vindicates God in showing mercy when judgment is in order. Through prayer and repentance we could see the re-shaping of the nations.

THE PRIVILEGE: OFFENSIVE PRAYING

Interceding to spare men and nations from judgment is a great responsibility. But there is also an aspect of privilege to intercession. God intends blessings and promises for His people. He has also bound Himself to give these in reponse to their prayers. "I will give you a new heart and put a new spirit in you" (Ezekiel 36:26, NIV).

He also said, "I will yet for this be enquired of by the house of Israel" (Verse 30, KJV). Two other translations read as follows:

> I am ready to hear Israel's prayers for these blessings, and to grant them their requests (LB).

> This also I will let the house of Israel ask me to do for them (RSV).

God plans to do it. He is waiting for men to ask Him. This helps us understand why we are told to ask of the Father (John 16:24, James 4:2) even though He already knows what we need (Matthew 6:8). S. D. Gordon, in *Quiet Talks on Prayer*, declared:

> Prayer surely does influence God. It does not influence His *purpose*. It does influence His *action*. Everything that ever has been prayed for, of course I mean every right thing, God has already purposed to do. But He does nothing without our consent. He has been hindered in His purposes by our lack of willingness. When we learn His purposes and make them our prayers we are giving Him the opportunity to act.[1] (Emphasis Added)

"Making his purposes our prayers" encompasses God's plan to use man as His instrument to accomplish His will on the earth. This was God's plan from the beginning (Genesis 1:26,28). Even after Adam defaulted, God continued to speak to individuals such as Moses and Abraham, revealing His will so they would know how to pray. Indeed, He must be true to His revealed character as stated in Amos 3:7: "Surely the Lord God will do nothing but he revealeth his secret unto His servants the prophets."

When a church begins to believe that they, through their prayers, become a base of operations through which God's will and Kingdom may be established in the earth (Luke 11:2), then they can say with gratitude and expectation, "It really does matter if we pray."

Note

1. S. D. Gordon, Quiet Talks on Prayer (New York: Grosset & Dunlap, 1941), pp. 58-59.

Part Five

Prayer Leadership

16

The Why, Who, and How of Leading in Corporate Prayer

THE WHY OF LEADERSHIP

Corporate prayer life must have dedicated, persistent leadership. People will not lead themselves to pray.

Finney said, "Unless the leader is especially prepared, the prayer meetings will dwindle."[1] This is a fact. Other church meetings can survive by dynamics, entertainment, or intellectual stimulation. But satan will not cease to try to hinder or conquer the prayer effort of the church! He does not care if we teach prayer, read about it, or talk about it. But when we actually pray, he marshals his forces against us. His two close allies, the flesh and the world, are constantly poised for their opportunity to strike.

In his book *The Weapon of Prayer*, E. M. Bounds said that if the devil can get the church to withdraw from prayer by believing reasonable excuses, the church is under his dominion.[2] "You need your rest. You are too busy doing good things. You must be balanced. Other things are important, too." What reasonable excuses these are! Time and time again we lay our laziness and selfishness upon the altar and watch unmoved as that sacrifice crawls off, while the Father's love grieves over our prodigal and fickle hearts.

The prayer leader must face these disheartening realities on a daily basis. As often as men gather to pray, the terrible trio of the world, the flesh, and the devil are there to rob them of their progress. This is why Jesus said, "Men ought always to pray and not to faint" (Luke 18:1). One translation reads ". . . and not cave in." We do cave in. We give up, go under, lose interest, forget, believe satan's lies, and sink into flesh-deadness. The struggle by nature is the flesh against the spirit and the spirit against the flesh (Galatians 5:17).

This is why we must have leadership, and the leadership must be especially prepared. Men desire to pray, but the flesh struggles against it. The place of leadership is to encourage and inspire, to teach, and to establish a framework for the prayer ministry of the church.

The leader is the vigilant helper of the purpose of God to establish corporate praying in the church. He is there to lift the shield of faith against the enemy's fiery darts. He is both an example and a teacher. He understands that he not only speaks to God, but he must also bring his brothers with him.

THE WHO OF LEADERSHIP

What leader does not have an empathy with the words of Paul, ". . . Who is sufficient for these things?" (II Corinthians 12:9) Leading prayer places a great spiritual demand upon the responsible individual. To be expected to accomplish daily tasks in the natural realm is one thing. Even to inspire men and teach them from an intellectual viewpoint is not unreasonable for some men. But to reach into heaven by faith and bring back answers in Jesus' name is a totally different consideration. And yet, of what value is prayer that does not produce answers or a prayer leader who does not inspire others to pray?

This is one of the highest callings on earth. The great prayer revival of 1858 was begun in America through the instigation of one man calling a prayer meeting with a few other men. Then several men began to do likewise. As little glowing coals came together to share their fervor, a sweeping fire of the Spirit covered the nation.

One evening Evan Roberts sat in a prayer meeting praying, "Lord, bend me, bend me." His experience of God's presence that night catapulted him into the leadership of one of the world's greatest revivals. Someone later said to him, "What if you had not been at that prayer meeting, Evan? Remember Thomas?" Roberts met God in this way because a faithful man kept coming to lead the prayer meeting.

The prayer leader must have a vision for birthing others into the reality that he himself has in prayer. Every praying person is not gifted to lead others in this way. Some intercessors do not make good prayer leaders, though they are good intercessors. Leading prayer is not only the ability to touch God's throne in prayer, but it is also the capacity to bring others with you.

Example.   Jesus' disciples desired to experience His quality of prayer life, so they requested, "Lord, teach us to pray." They liked what they saw. They knew it was real. They observed His consistency and the results in His life in terms of miracles and power. What they saw was His relationship with His Father—a life of obedience to the will of God that formed the basis of Jesus' character.

There are gifts of leadership in varying areas, but gifted individuals never go far unless they develop the character to support their gift. One may be gifted in the area of prayer, but others will not follow him unless in his life he is consistently obedient to the Lordship of Jesus Christ. His own prayer life must be one after which to pattern. He need not be a Brainerd or a Payson, but he must be one who is disciplined, sincere, and who knows how to pray and receive answers.

Spiritual Life.   The single most important attribute of the prayer leader is *life*. There are many contributing virtues, but without the life of the Spirit, a person can never lead successfully. We have individuals in our prayer meetings who consistently pray a life-giving sound. They may only read out a short Scripture, but it will be alive and will raise the spiritual level of the prayer meeting. We consider to be true prayer leaders in our church those who are gifted to infuse life into the prayer meeting. This will be the result of their taking the responsibility to vocalize the living relationship they have with the Lord, while they have a concern for the general well-being and success of each prayer meeting. All who pray with this unction contribute to leading in prayer, supporting the one who has the oversight of the gathering.

The Holy Spirit is a quickening Spirit (Romans 8:11). The life He gives is supernatural. It may be imitated, but it can never be duplicated. It is not found in dynamics, volume, or excitement. It is a true power given of God, gained through prayer and time in the Word.

Discernment. Leaders must take responsibility concerning the direction of the prayer meeting; either to allow it to follow the direction it is taking or to take measures to redirect it. The leader must be able to ascertain the will of God for that particular meeting. Trying to accomplish this by a set plan or through an intellectual approach is disastrous to the life of the meeting.

Spiritual discernment is definitely a gift (I Corinthians 12:10). It is also developed by training and experience (Hebrews 5:14). It is the ability to distinguish, especially in spiritual realms, but also relating to practical circumstances. Ultimately, it means the person is capable of knowing what should or should not happen in a prayer meeting.

THE HOW OF LEADERSHIP

Awareness is a key word. Finney has said that if the leader prays far beyond the people, they will be repulsed.[3] Knowing who the people are and ascertaining the spiritual climate of the gathering will put the leader in touch with what they can achieve in prayer.

When I lead, I try to allow my spirit to listen to the people as well as to the voice of God. The idea is not to get them to pray what I think they should, but to give them room and then redirect according to the Spirit's leading. There are many ways to gently guide and focus a prayer meeting. Sometimes I lead a song to lift a heavy meeting, to express a need, or to give praise for a victory. People can sometimes be gathered through a song better than by speaking; the song can stir faith, melt hearts, and express gratitude. The reading of a Scripture is another very powerful way for a leader to interject life or introduce a subject for prayer. Then he or someone else can pray on the Scripture he has just read, developing a flow for the meeting.

Intensity and zeal are required to keep the prayer meeting on course. Again, this is a very spiritual ministry and cannot be preplanned or accomplished through an intellectual approach. Henry Ward Beecher has a novel way of picturing the leader's position:

> "You have got to drive prayer-meetings just as you do horses. You cannot keep flies from biting them, nor them from whisking their tails, in a summer's day. You have got to make the best of your annoyances."[4]

Such responsibility calls for alertness, energy, concentration, and a willingness to take authority when necessary. It requires much private prayer and study of the Word in preparation to reach a fine balance between aggressively directing and giving room for liberty.

Successful prayer leading demands great patience. We cannot be censorious or legalistic in our approach, but willing to be tried and inconvenienced by the blunderings or inabilities of those praying. The Scripture says to "pour out your heart before Him" (Psalms 62:8). That can be done in a variety of ways, all acceptable to the Lord when done in the right spirit. We must pray to be able to discern what is pleasing to God, rather than please our own notions.

Prayer leadership must also be attended by gentleness. Kindness must find its place in our mouths as a law (Proverbs 31:26). People will feel secure, even willing to make mistakes, if they know their leader is committed to kind speaking. This does not mean we should not correct. But abruptness is selfishness and unwillingness to pay the price of patience and kindness. A person with a harsh manner has not earned the right to lead prayer meetings.

The leader also takes the responsibility of closing the meeting. It may be closed with a prayer, a song, or a simple amen, but few people know the right time to close it. These are some general guidelines to help in this area.

1) The leader should close the meeting before the unction of the Spirit and interest of the people begin to wane. If the life of the meeting is spent, the people will be left with a negative impression and will not look forward to the next meeting for prayer.

2) The leader should be definite. If someone prays another prayer after he has closed the meeting, he should close it again immediately after that prayer. People will continue to try to pray when he is endeavoring to close the meeting. He should not become frustrated by this. The praying has opened the spiritual atmosphere so the people now feel more free even though the spirit of prayer has lifted from the meeting. The leader should close the meeting anyway when he feels it is time to do so.

3) The leader should set the example of reverence following a prayer meeting. Even if it ended on a joyful or victorious note, it is not a time for joking and loud talking.

The successful prayer leader must be both acutely spiritual and sensibly practical. Giftings of leadership may be developed through study and instruction, but only the discipline of private prayer and time in the Word produce the sensitivity to support this responsibility.

There is no greater blessing—and no greater challenge—than leading a congregation in prayer; but the Lord has promised, "My grace is sufficient for thee" (II Corinthians 12:9). A song written by one of our members aptly expresses the heart cry of those seeking to serve in this realm.

> Make me worthy of the high calling;
> Make me worthy to run the race.
> Break me often, come and soften
> My stony heart to receive your grace.

Notes

1. Charles Grandison Finney, *Finney on Revival* (Minneapolis, Minnesota: Bethany Fellowship, Inc.), p. 52.
2. E. M. Bounds, *The Weapon of Prayer* (Grand Rapids, Michigan: Dickinson Brothers, Inc., 1975), p. 14.
3. Charles Grandison Finney, *Finney on Revival* (Minneapolis, Minnesota: Bethany Fellowship, Inc.) p. 52.
4. Henry Ward Beecher, *Yale Lectures on Preaching* (New York: Fords, Howard, and Hulbert, 1893).

Conclusion

God loves His Church too much to let it flounder in crippled, albeit sincere, efforts to see His purpose established in the earth. In His mercy He has always issued a fresh challenge to the Church when it begins to wane in zeal and direction. His grace inspires us with new desire to obey and please Him.

We have reclaimed the truths of salvation, the work of the Holy Spirit, and worship in Spirit and in truth. Now He is restoring prayer to His Church by sending His Word and His Spirit to teach and establish His people in corporate praying.

Just as God calls every Christian to communion with Himself through prayer, He also calls every church to be a praying force to accomplish His will in the earth. He has promised to do things through the agreeing prayers of the Church that He will not do through the prayers of individuals.

The Scriptures and historical testimony witness that the power of God is released through the prayers of the saints to affect the will of God. We can pray with confidence that we will accomplish His purposes on the earth. Every church becomes a base of operations for "Thy Kingdom come . . . in earth."

As leadership and congregation join hearts and hands to this end, our churches can be restored to vital communion with God which manifests itself in power and direction. Once again the praying Church will arise against the enemies of God and bring to bear the victory of Calvary.

For a complete list of tapes and books by Sue Curran write:

Shekinah Church Ministries
394 Glory Road
Blountville, TN 37617